FOR ALL ELECTRONIC KEYBOARDS

Easy ELECTRONIC KEYBOARD MUSIC

ELTON JOHN ANTHOLOGY

151

Hal Leonard
Publishing
Corporation

7777 West Bluemound Road
P.O. Box 13819 Milwaukee, WI 53213

ELTON JOHN ANTHOLOGY

Contents

All The Girls Love Alice

Regi-Sound Program: 5
Rhythm: Rock

Words and Music by
Elton John and Taupin

Raised to be a la - dy by the gold - en rule.
al - i - ty it seems _____ was just a dream.

She Al - ice was the spawn _____ of a
could - n't get it on _____ with the

pub - lic school. With a dou - ble bar - rel
boys on the scene. But _____ what do you ex -

name _____ in the back of her brain. And a
pect from a chick who's just six - teen _____ And _____

sim - ple case of "Mum - my does - n't love me" blues.

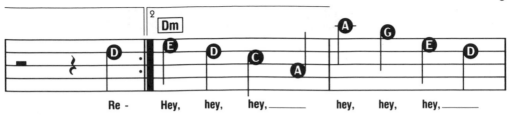

Re - Hey, hey, hey, _____ hey, hey, hey, _____

hey. You know what I mean.

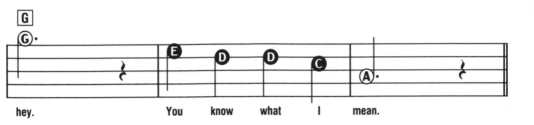

All the young girls love Al - ice. Ten - der young Al - ice they

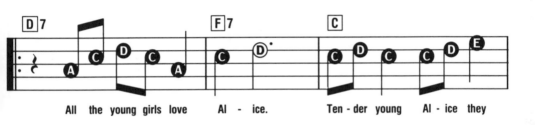

{ say. Come o - ver and see _____ me, come o - ver and please _ me.
{ say. If I give you my num - ber will you prom - ise to call _____ me.

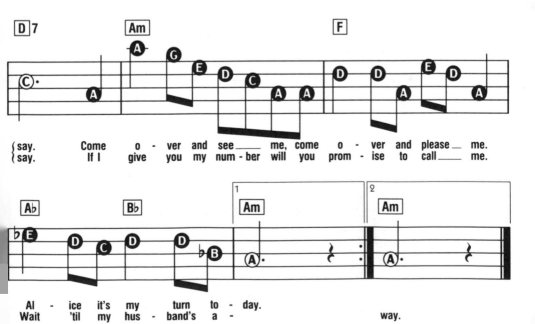

Al - ice it's my turn to - day.
Wait 'til my hus - band's a - way.

Ball & Chain

Regi-Sound Program: 6
Rhythm: Rock

Words and Music by
Elton John and Gary Osborne

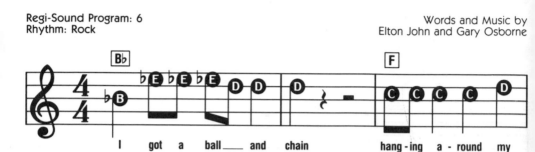

I got a ball___ and chain hang-ing a-round my

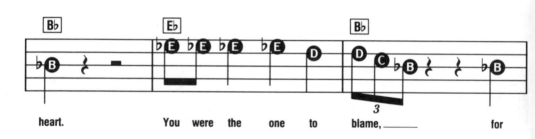

heart. You were the one to blame,___ for

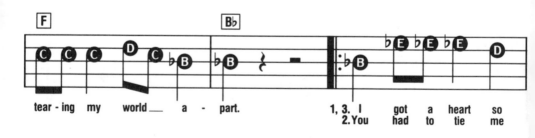

tear-ing my world___ a - part. 1, 3. I got a heart so
2. You had to tie me

true,   you   got   a   heart___ of   ice.   A
down   in - side a cage___ of doubt.   I'm

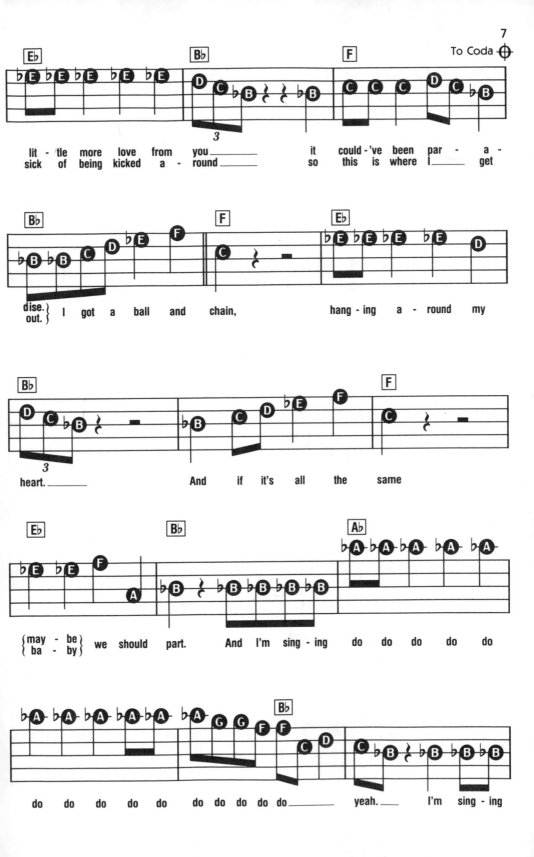

To Coda ⊕

lit - tle more love from you_____ it could - 've been par - a -
sick of being kicked a - round_____ so this is where I_____ get

dise.⎞
out.⎠ I got a ball and chain, hang - ing a - round my

heart._____ And if it's all the same

{may - be}
{ba - by} we should part. And I'm sing - ing do do do do do

do do do do do do do do do do_____ yeah._____ I'm sing - ing

8

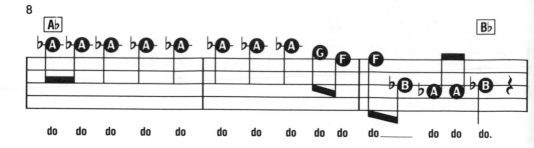

do do do do do do do do do do do_____ do do do.

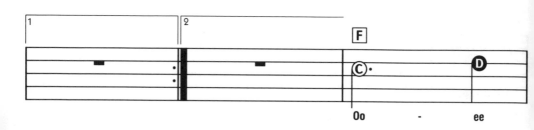

Oo - ee

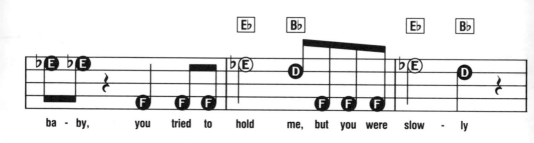

ba - by, you tried to hold me, but you were slow - ly

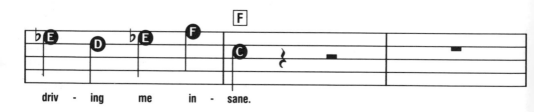

driv - ing me in - sane.

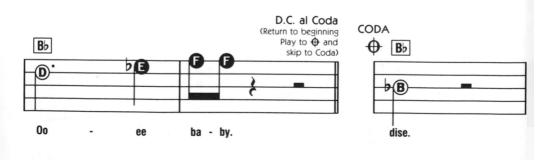

Oo - ee ba - by.

dise.

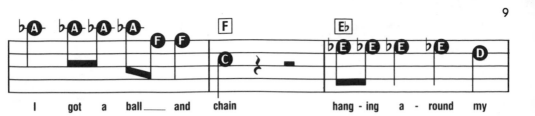

I got a ball___ and chain hang-ing a-round my

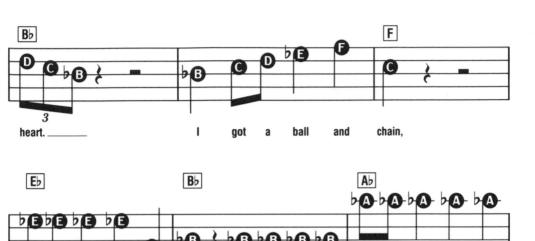

heart.___ I got a ball and chain,

hang-ing a-round my heart. And I'm sing-ing do do do do do

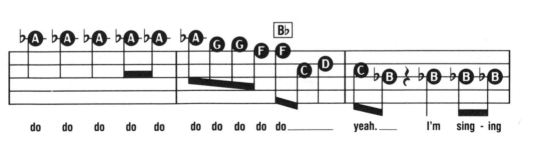

do do do do do do do do do do___ yeah.___ I'm sing-ing

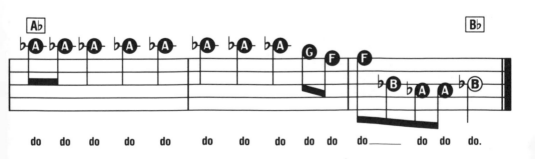

do do do do do do do do do do do___ do do do.

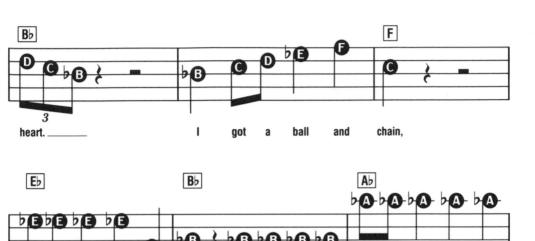

9

Bennie And The Jets

Regi-Sound Program: 4
Rhythm: Rock

Words and Music by
Elton John and Taupin

Hey   kids   shake it loose to - geth - er the
Hey   kids   plug in - to the faith -   less

spot - lights hit - ting some - thing that's been known to change the weath - er
may - be   they're   blind - ed   but Ben - nie makes them age - less

We'll   kill   the   fat - ted   calf   to - night   so   stick a -
We shall   sur - vive   let   us take   our - selves

round   You're gon - na hear e - lec - tric
a - long   Where we fight our par - ents out in the

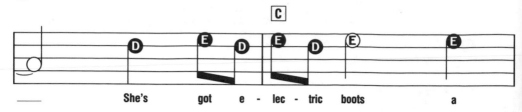

She's got e - lec - tric boots a

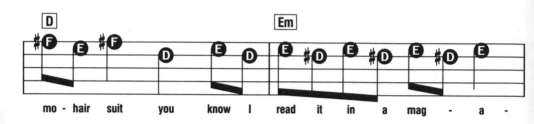

mo - hair suit you know I read it in a mag - a -

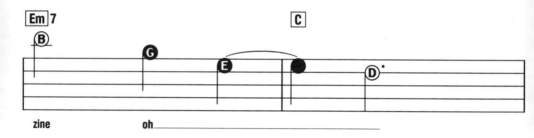

zine oh_____

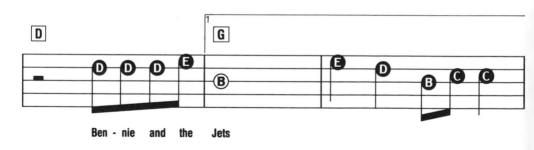

Ben - nie and the Jets

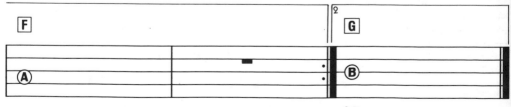

Jets

Bite Your Lip
(Get Up And Dance)

Regi-Sound Program: 7
Rhythm: Rock

Words and Music by
Elton John and Taupin

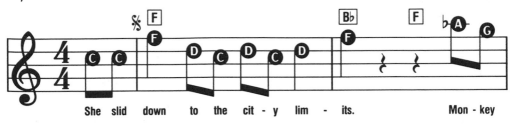

She slid down to the cit - y lim - its. Mon - key

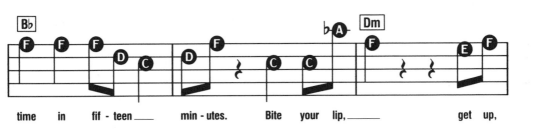

time in fif - teen ___ min - utes. Bite your lip, ___ get up,

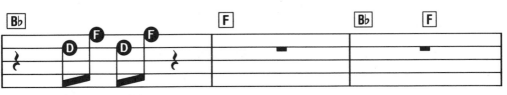

get up and dance.

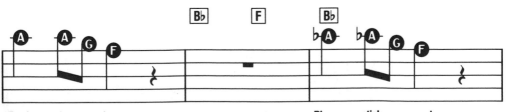

Don't let me down. Please stick a - round.

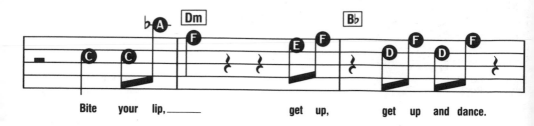

Bite your lip,_____ get up, get up and dance.

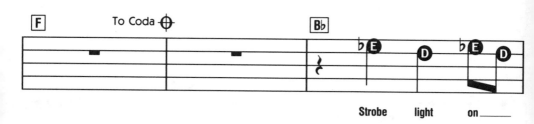

Strobe light on_____

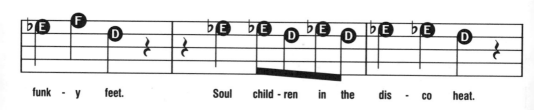

funk - y feet. Soul child - ren in the dis - co heat.

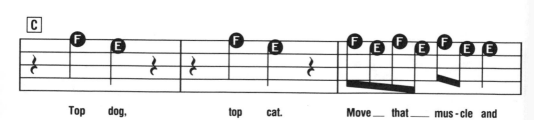

Top dog, top cat. Move__ that__ mus - cle and

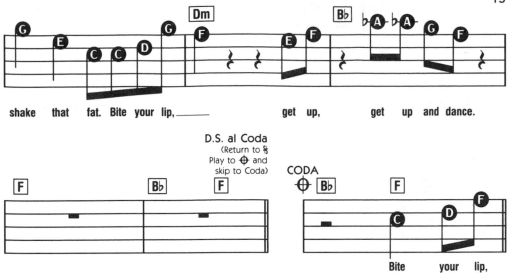

shake that fat. Bite your lip, _____ get up, get up and dance.

D.S. al Coda
(Return to %
Play to ⊕ and
skip to Coda)

CODA

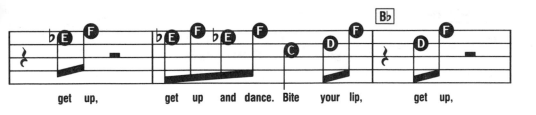

Bite your lip,

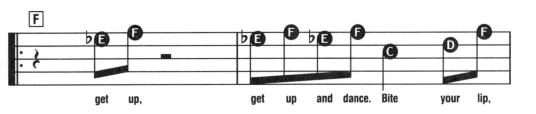

get up, get up and dance. Bite your lip,

get up, get up and dance. Bite your lip, get up,

Repeat and Fade

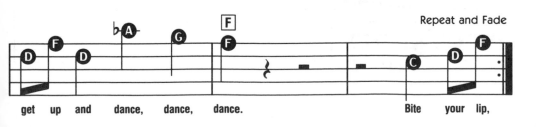

get up and dance, dance, dance. Bite your lip,

The Bitch Is Back

Regi-Sound Program: 5
Rhythm: Rock

Words and Music by
Elton John and Taupin

I was jus - ti - fied___ when I was five, rais - in' cane I spit in your eye. Times are chang - in' now the poor get___ fat, but the fe - ver's gon - na catch you when the bitch gets back.___ Eat meat on Fri - day that's al - right. I

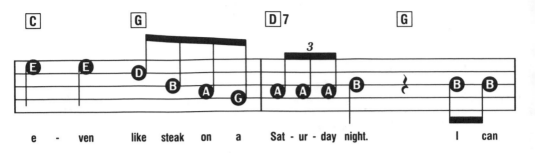

e - ven like steak on a Sat - ur - day night. I can

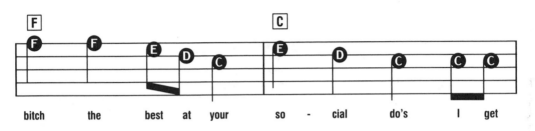

bitch the best at your so - cial do's I get

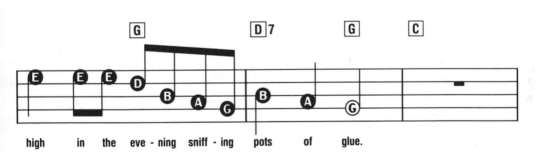

high in the eve - ning sniff - ing pots of glue.

I'm a bitch, I'm a bitch, oh the bitch is_____ back.

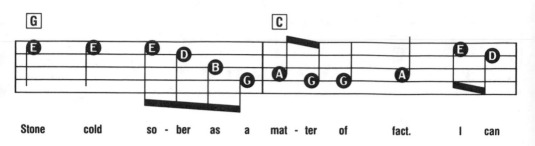

Stone   cold   so - ber   as   a   mat - ter   of   fact.   I   can

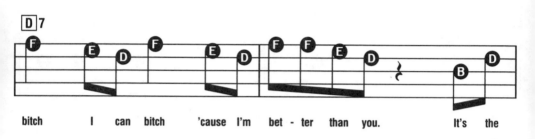

bitch   I   can   bitch   'cause I'm   bet - ter   than   you.   It's   the

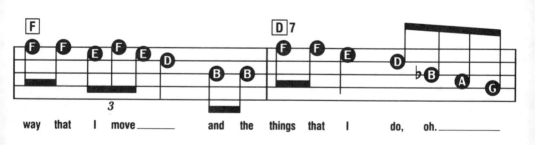

way   that   I   move_____   and   the   things   that   I   do,   oh._____

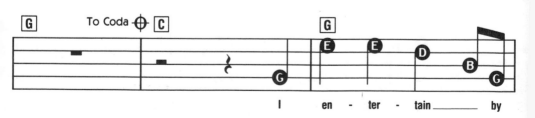

I   en - ter - tain_____ by

pick - ing brains.   Sell   my   soul _____ by   drop - ping names.   I

don't   like   those! ___   My   God,   what's   that!   Oh, it's

full   of   nast - y   hab - its   when the   bitch   gets   back.

D.S. al Coda
(Return to 𝄋
Play to ⊕ and
skip to Coda)

CODA

I'm   a

Bitch,   bitch,

Repeat and Fade

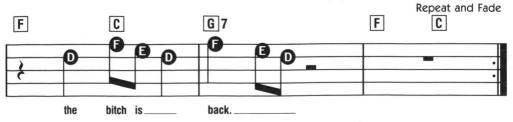

the   bitch is _____ back. _____

Blue Eyes

Regi-Sound Program: 1
Rhythm: Ballad

Words and Music by
Elton John and Gary Osborne

Border Song

Regi-Sound Program: 6
Rhythm: Ballad

Words and Music by
Elton John and Taupin

1. Ho - ly Mo - ses_____ I have been re - moved_____
2. Ho - ly Mo - ses_____ I have been de - ceived_____
3. *(see additional lyrics)*

I have seen the spec - tre he has__ been here__ too.
Now the wind has changed di - rec - tion and I__ have to__ leave.

Dis - tant cous - in from down the line____ brand of peo ple who ain't my kind_____
Won't you please__ ex - cuse my frank - ness__ but it's not__ my cup of tea._____

To Coda ⊕

__ Ho - ly Mo - ses____ I have been re - moved_____
Ho - ly Mo - ses____ I have been de - ceived_____

3. Holy Moses Let us live in peace,
   Let us strive to find a way
   to make all hatred cease.
   There's a man over there,
   What's his color I don't care,
   He's my brother, Let us live in peace.
   Oh he's my brother let us live in peace.

Burn Down The Mission

Regi-Sound Program: 6
Rhythm: 8 Beat or Pops

Words and Music by
Elton John and Taupin

You tell me there's an an-gel in your tree,_____
woods the squir-rels are___ out to-day,_____

did he say he'd come to call on me?_____
my wife cried when they came to take me a-way.___

For things are get-ting des-p'rate in our home,_____ liv-ing in the
But what more could I do just to keep her warm_____ than

par-ish_____ of the rest-less folks I_____ know.___ } Ev-'ry-bod-y now,
burn,___ burn, burn, burn down the mis-sion walls._____

25

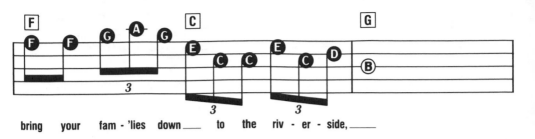

bring your fam - 'lies down___ to the riv - er - side, ___

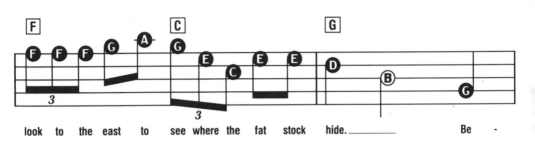

look to the east to see where the fat stock hide. ___ Be -

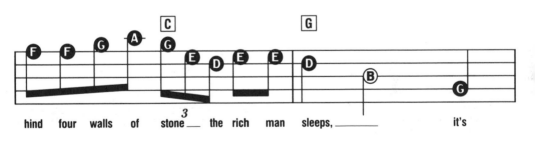

hind four walls of stone___ the rich man sleeps, ___ it's

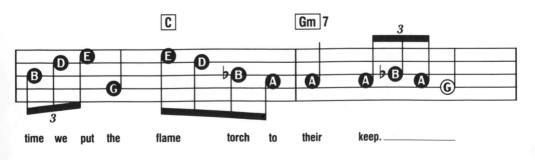

time we put the flame torch to their keep. ___

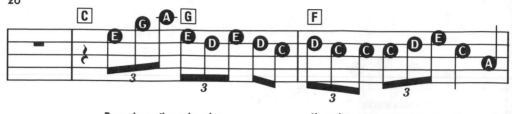

Burn down the mis-sion _____ If we're gon-na stay a-live, ____

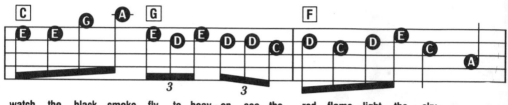

watch the black smoke fly to heav-en, see the red flame light the sky. _____

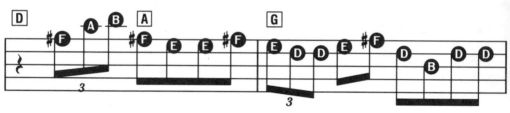

Burn down the mis-sion, burn it down __ to stay a-live, ____ it's our

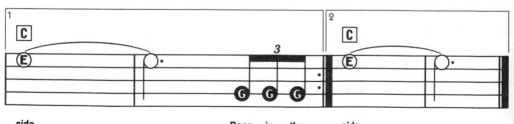

on-ly chance of liv-ing, take all you need _____ to live in -

side. _____ Deep in the side. _____

Candle In The Wind

Regi-Sound Program: 8
Rhythm: Medium Rock

Words and Music by
Elton John and Taupin

Good - bye, Nor - ma Jean. _____ the Though I nev - er
Lone - li - ness was tough, _____ the tough - est role _____

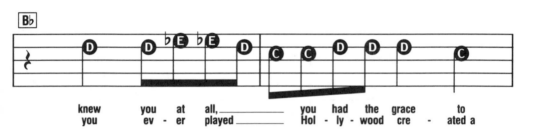

knew you at all, _____ you had the grace to
you ev - er played _____ Hol - ly - wood cre - ated a

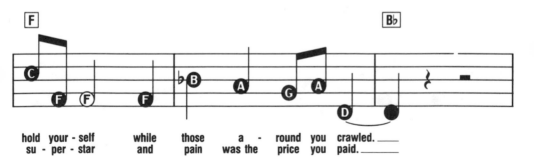

hold your - self while those a - round you crawled. _____
su - per - star and pain was the price you paid. _____

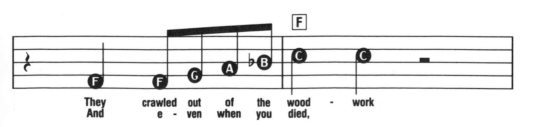

They crawled out of the wood - work
And e - ven when you died,

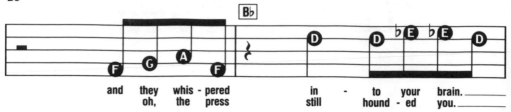

and they whis-pered in - to your brain._____
oh, the press still hound-ed you._____

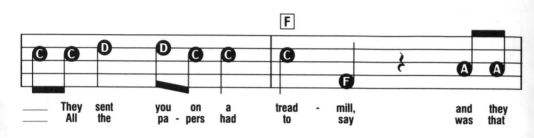

_____ They sent you on a tread - mill, and they
All the pa - pers had to say was that

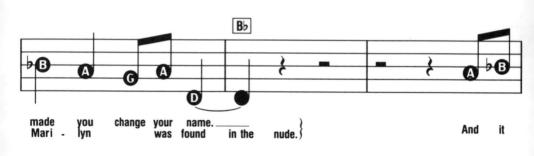

made you change your name._____ And it
Mari - lyn was found in the nude.

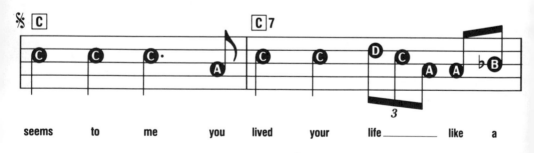

seems to me you lived your life_____ like a

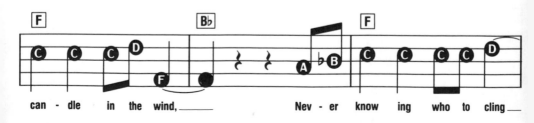

can - dle in the wind,_____ Nev - er know ing who to cling_____

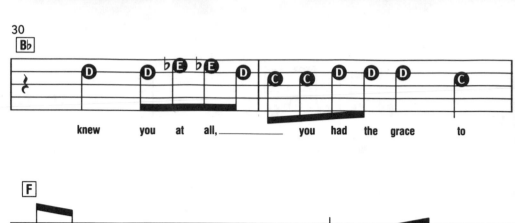

knew you at all, _____ you had the grace to

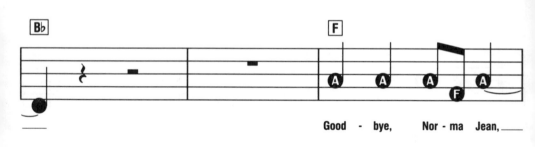

hold your - self while those a - round you crawled. _____

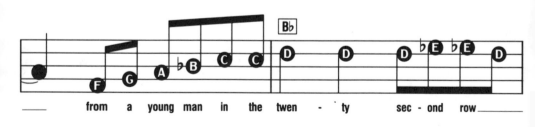

Good - bye, Nor - ma Jean, ____

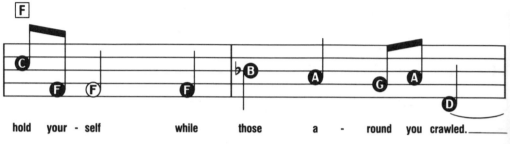

____ from a young man in the twen - ty sec - ond row _____

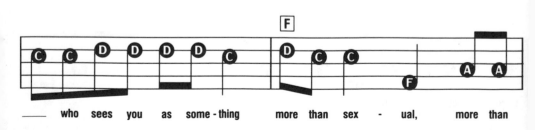

____ who sees you as some - thing more than sex - ual, more than

31
D.S. al Coda
(Return to %
Play to ⊕ and
skip to Coda)

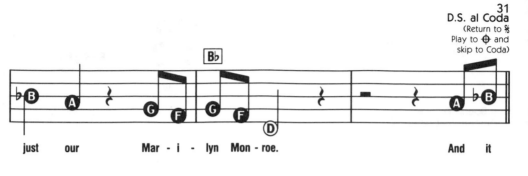

just   our   Mar - i - lyn Mon - roe.   And   it

CODA

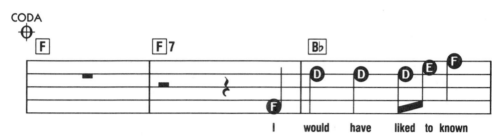

I   would   have   liked to known

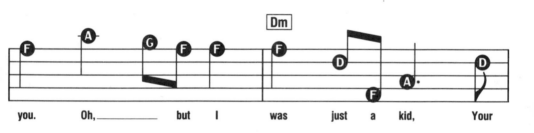

you.   Oh,____   but   I   was   just   a   kid,   Your

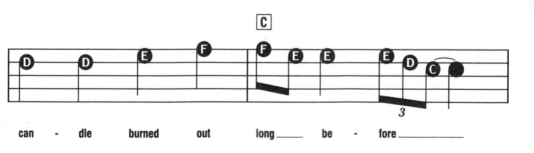

can - dle   burned   out   long____ be - fore____

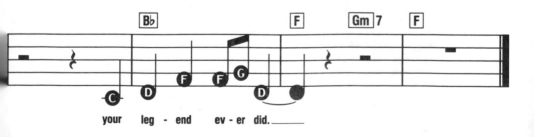

your   leg - end   ev - er did.____

Captain Fantastic
And The Brown Dirt Cowboy

Regi-Sound Program: 8
Rhythm: 8 Beat or Pops

Words and Music by
Elton John and Taupin

Cap - tain Fan - tas - tic, raised and reg - i - ment - ed.
While little Dirt Cow - boys turned brown in their sad - dles.

Hard - ly a he - ro. Just some - one his moth - er might know,
Sweet choc' - late bis - cuits, and red ros - y ap - ples in sum -

mer. For it's ver - y clear - ly a case for
 hay make and "hey mom.

corn - flakes and clas - sics. "Two teas both with sug - ar
do the pa - pers say any - thing good." Are there chances in life for

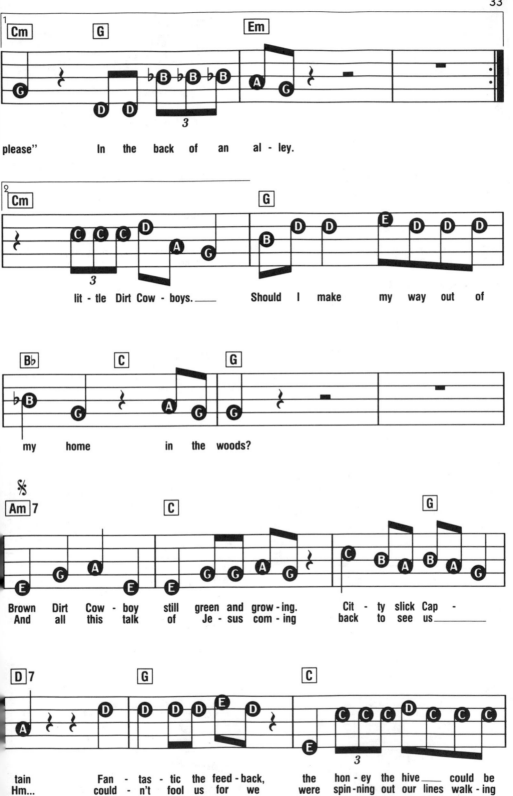

Chloe

Regi-Sound Program: 10
Rhythm: 8 Beat or Pops

Words and Music by
Elton John and Gary Osborne

How come you're so un-der-stand - in'_____
How you han - dle what you live through _____
You're the life - line that I cling to_____

when I tell you all my lies,_____
I can nev - er hope to learn,_____
when I feel like giv - in' in,_____

and pre -
tak - in'
when the

tend - in' to be-lieve them, _____
all the pain I give you, _____
dreams that I re - ly on_____

38

Country Comfort

Regi-Sound Program: 10
Rhythm: 8 Beat or Pops

Words and Music by
Elton John and Taupin

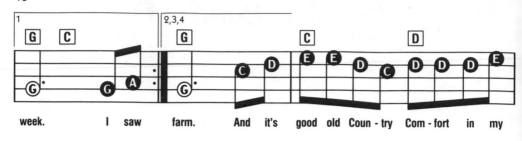

week.   I saw   farm.   And it's good old Coun - try Com - fort in my

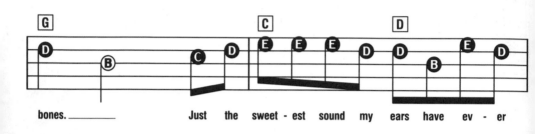

bones. _____   Just the sweet - est sound my ears have ev - er

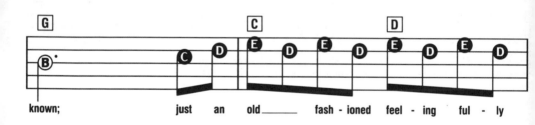

known;   just an old_____ fash - ioned feel - ing ful - ly

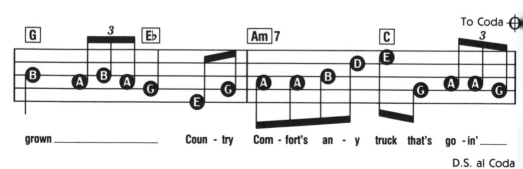

grown _____   Coun - try Com - fort's an - y truck that's go - in'_____

D.S. al Coda
(Return to %
Play to ⊕ and
skip to Coda)

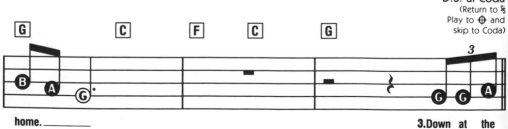

home. _____   3.Down at   the
                                              4. Now the

41

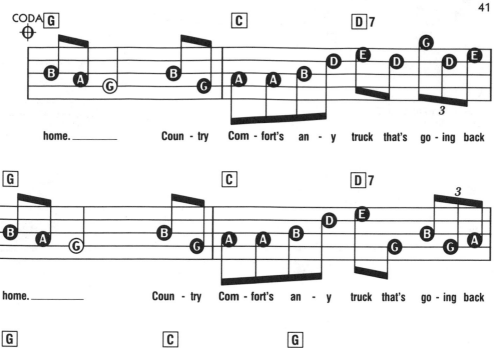

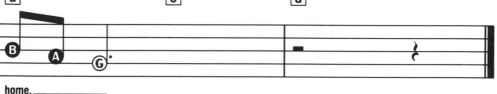

home. _____

3. **Down at the well they've got a new machine,
Foreman says it cuts manpower by fifteen,
But that ain't natural, so old Clay would say,
He's a horse-drawn man until his dying day.**

(Repeat Chorus)

4. **Now the old fat goose is flying 'cross the sticks,
The hedge-hog's done in clay between the bricks,
And the rocking chair's a-creaking on the porch,
Across the valley moves the herdsman with his torch.**

(Repeat Chorus)

Crocodile Rock

Regi-Sound Program: 5
Rhythm: Rock

Words and Music by
Elton John and Taupin

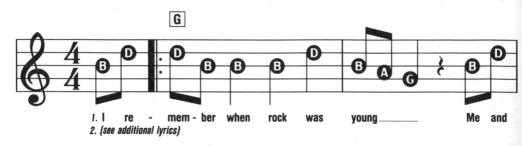

1. I re - mem - ber when rock was young_____ Me and
2. (see additional lyrics)

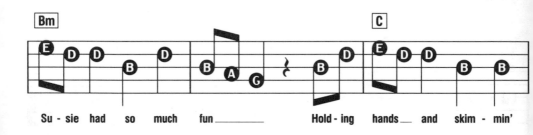

Su - sie had so much fun_____ Hold - ing hands___ and skim - min'

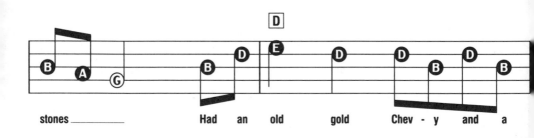

stones_____ Had an old gold Chev - y and a

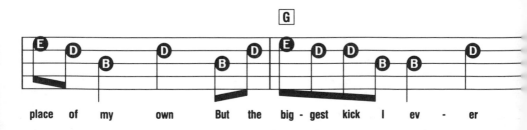

place of my own But the big - gest kick I ev - er

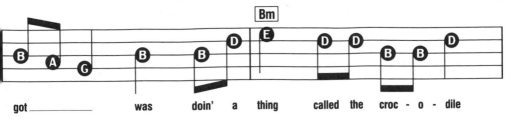

got _____ was doin' a thing called the croc - o - dile

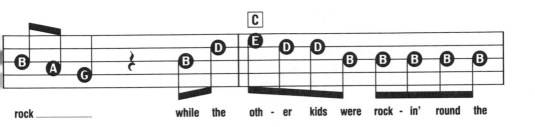

rock _____ while the oth - er kids were rock - in' round the

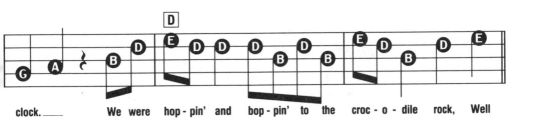

clock. ___ We were hop - pin' and bop - pin' to the croc - o - dile rock, Well

Chorus

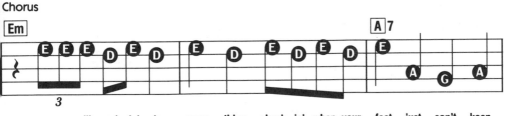

croc - o - dile rock - in' is some - thing shock - in' when your feet just can't keep

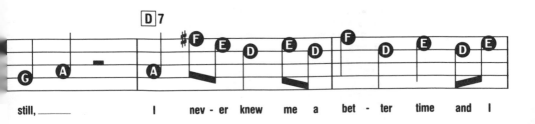

still, _____ I nev - er knew me a bet - ter time and I

44

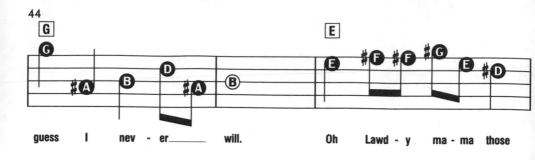

guess I nev - er_____ will. Oh Lawd - y ma - ma those

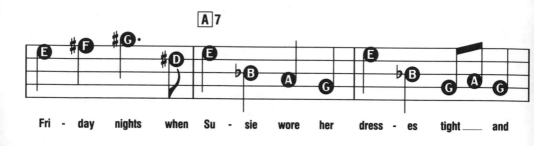

Fri - day nights when Su - sie wore her dress - es tight____ and

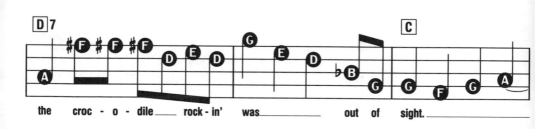

the croc - o - dile____ rock - in' was_____ out of sight._____

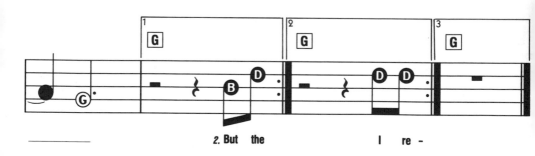

_____ 2. But the I re -

2. (But the) years went by and rock just died
   Susie went and left us for some foreign guy.
   Long nights cryin' by the record machine
   dreamin' of my Chevy and my old blue jeans.
   But they'll never kill the thrills we've got
   burning up to the crocodile rock
   learning fast as the weeks went past
   We really thought the crocodile rock would last, Well
   (to chorus)

Daniel

Regi-Sound Program: 2
Rhythm: Latin or Rock

Words and Music by
Elton John and Taupin

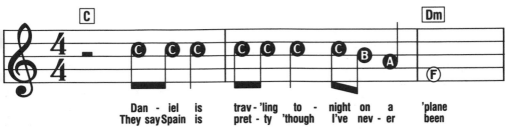

Dan - iel   is   trav - 'ling to - night on a   'plane
They say Spain is   pret - ty 'though I've nev - er   been

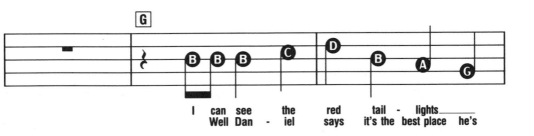

I can see   the   red   tail - lights_____
Well Dan - iel   says   it's the best place he's

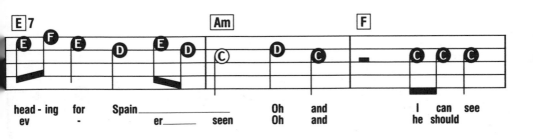

head - ing for   Spain_____   Oh and   I can see
ev -   er____ seen   Oh and   he should

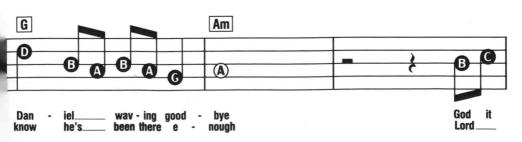

Dan - iel____ wav - ing good - bye   God it
know   he's____ been there e - nough   Lord____

46

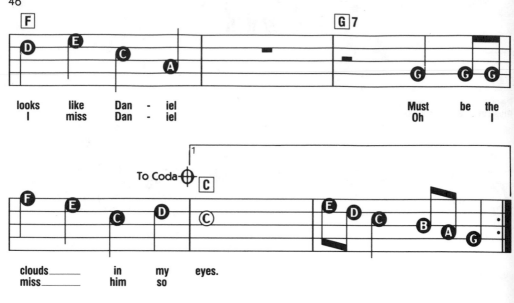

looks   like   Dan - iel   Must   be   the
I   miss   Dan - iel   Oh   I

To Coda

clouds_____   in   my   eyes.
miss_____   him   so

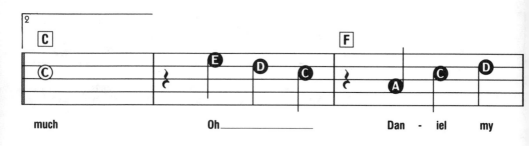

much   Oh_____   Dan - iel   my

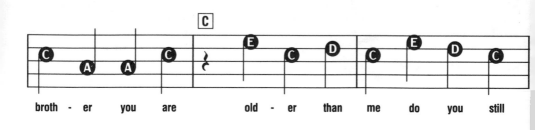

broth - er   you   are   old - er   than   me   do   you   still

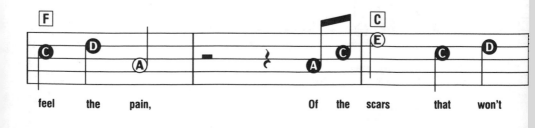

feel   the   pain,   Of   the   scars   that   won't

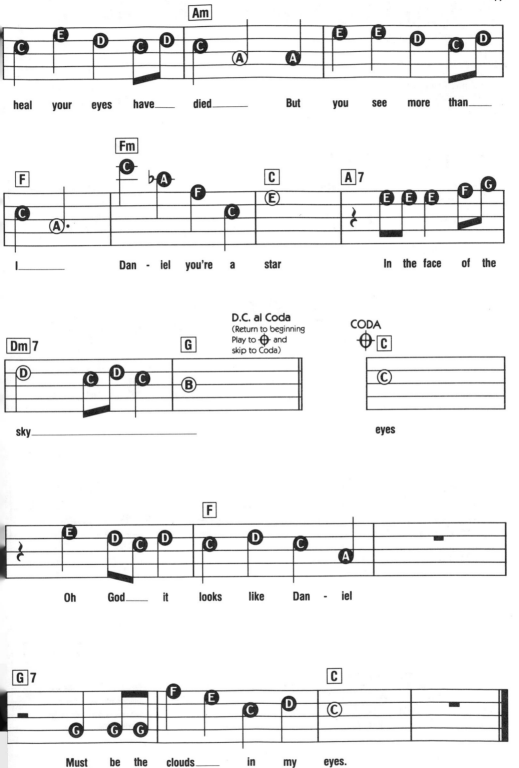

heal your eyes have___ died___ But you see more than___

Dan - iel you're a star In the face of the

D.C. al Coda
(Return to beginning
Play to ⊕ and
skip to Coda)

CODA
⊕ C

sky___

eyes

Oh God___ it looks like Dan - iel

Must be the clouds___ in my eyes.

Don't Go Breaking My Heart

Regi-Sound Program: 1
Rhythm: Ballad

Words and Music by
Carte Blanche and Ann Orson

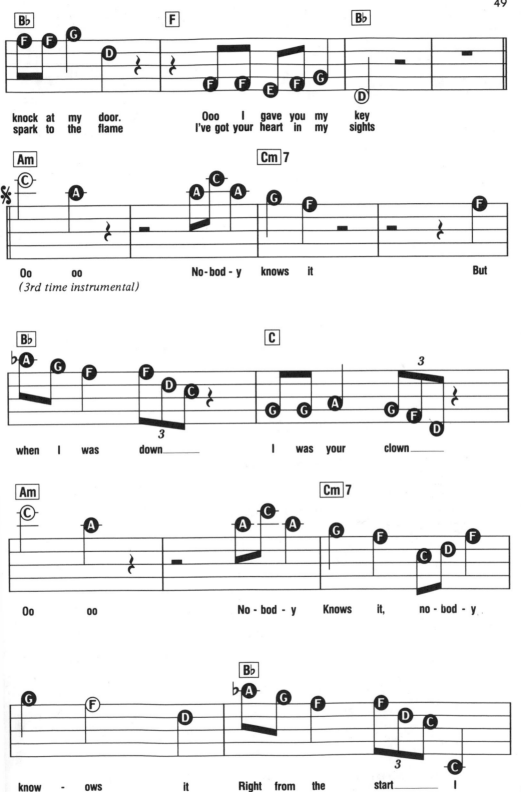

50

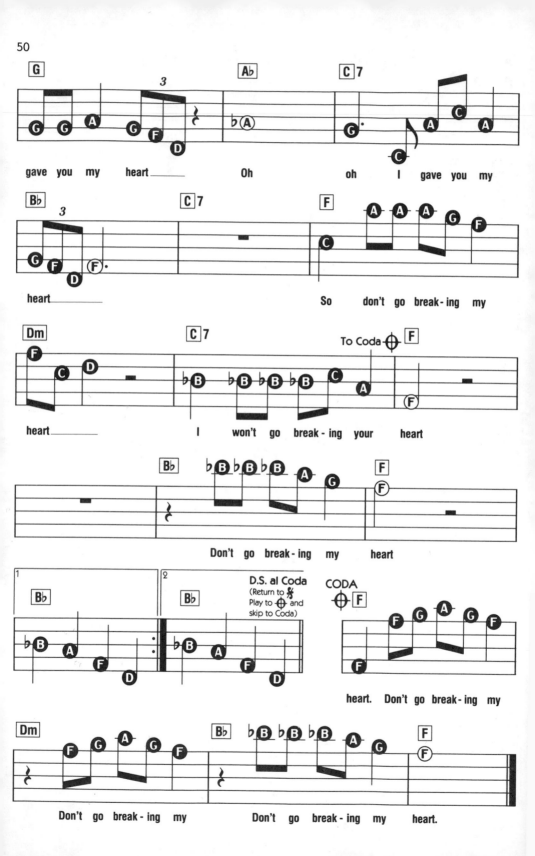

Funeral For A Friend

Regi-Sound Program: 5
Rhythm: March or Slow Rock

Words and Music by
Elton John and Taupin

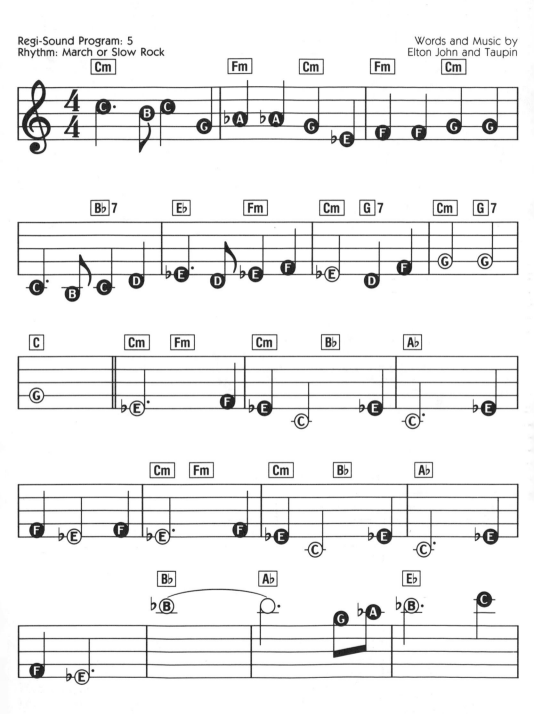

52

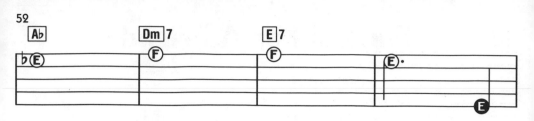

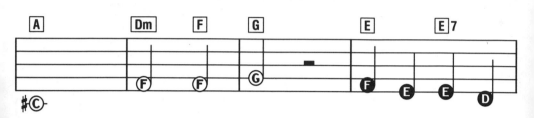

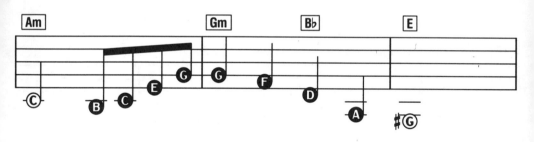

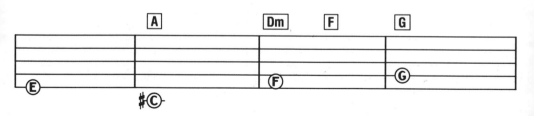

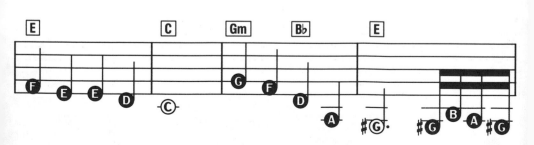

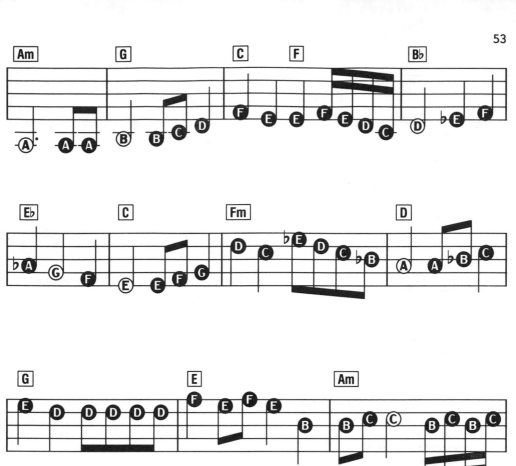

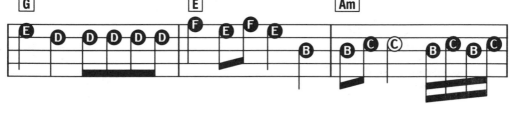

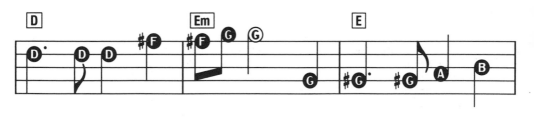

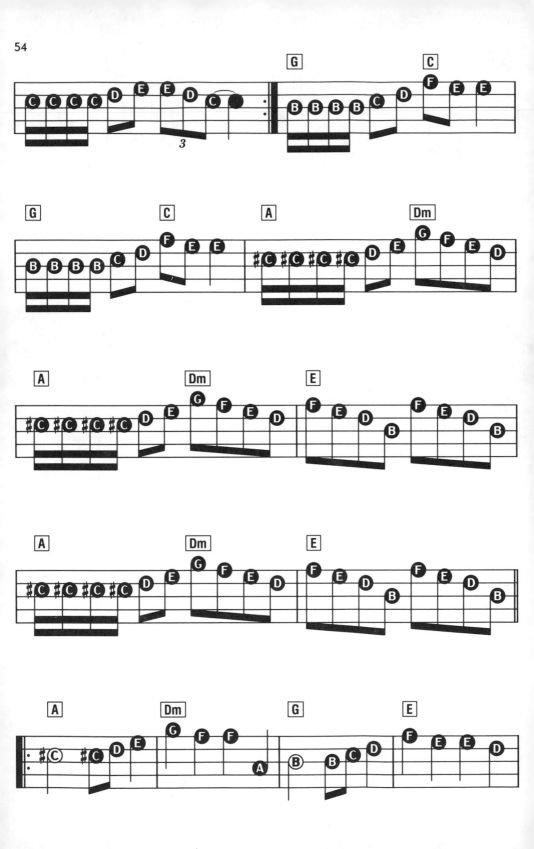

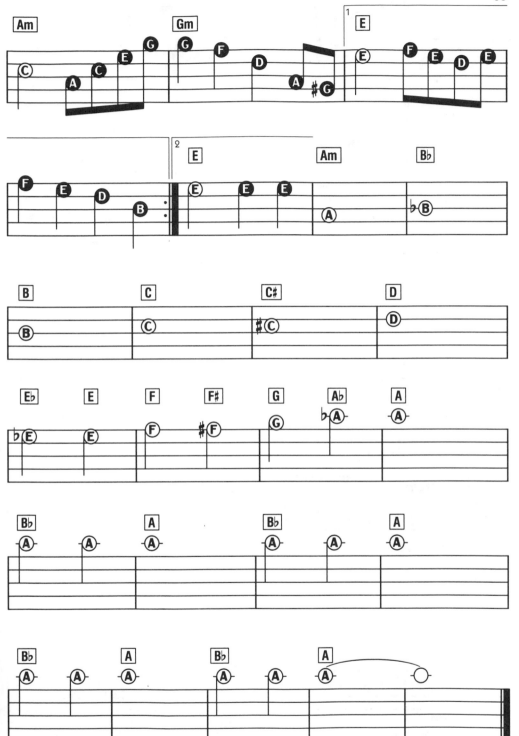

Don't Let The Sun Go Down On Me

Regi-Sound Program: 4
Rhythm: Rock

Words and Music by
Elton John and Taupin

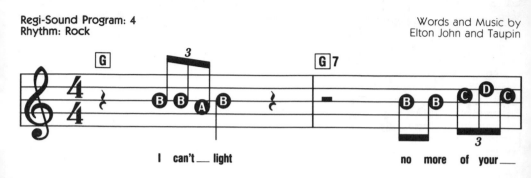

I can't _ light no more of your _

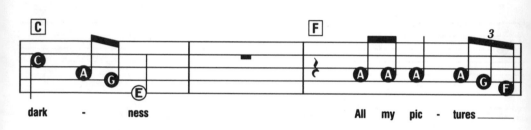

dark - ness All my pic - tures _

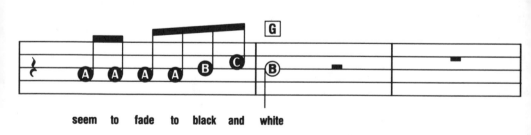

seem to fade to black and white

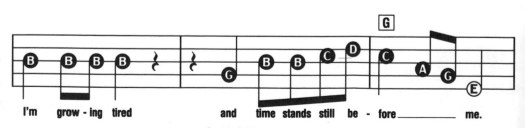

I'm grow - ing tired and time stands still be - fore _ me.

57

Empty Garden
(Hey Hey Johnny)

Regi-Sound Program: 4
Rhythm: Ballad

Words and Music by
Elton John and Taupin

lived   here?_____   He   must   have   been   a   gar - den - er   who
lived   there?_____   He   must   have   been   a   gar - den - er   who

cared   a   lot,   who   weed - ed   out   the   tears   and   grew   a
cared   a   lot,   who   weed - ed   out   the   tears   and   grew   a

good_____   crop,   And   we   are   so   a - mazed,   we're
good_____   crop,   Now   we   pray   for   rain,   And with

crip - pled   and   we're   dazed._____   A   gar - den er   like   that   one.____
ev - 'ry   drop   that   pours,_____   we   hear,____

no   one   can   re - place.____}   And   I've   been   knock - ing,
we   hear your   name. ____}

but   no   one   an - swers,   And   I've   been   knock - ing

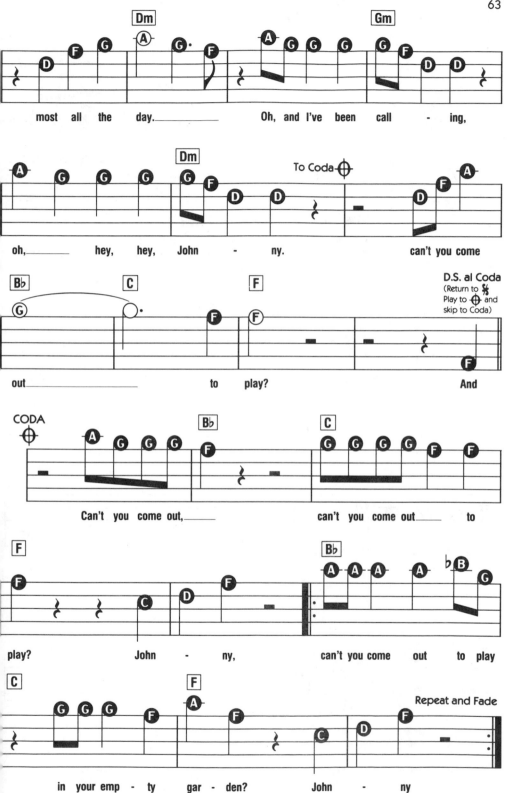

Friends

Regi-Sound Program: 4
Rhythm: 8 Beat or Pops

Words and Music by
Elton John and Taupin

Mak - ing friends _____ for the world __ to see,

let the peo - ple know you got what you need.

With a friend at hand __ you will see the light, if your

friends are there __ then ev - er - y - thing's all right. _____ It

right. _____

right. _____

La, la, la, la, la, la, la, la, la.

Goodbye Yellow Brick Road

Regi-Sound Program: 5
Rhythm: Slow Rock

Words and Music by
Elton John and Taupin

Dm | **A** | **B♭**

Back to the howl - ing old owl in the woods Hunt - ing the horn - y back

D♭ | **F**

toad Oh I've fin' - ly de - cid - ed my

Dm | **B♭** | **C 7** | **D♭**

fu - ture lies Be - yond the yel - low brick road_____

E♭ | **A♭** | **D♭** | **B♭m**

_____ Ah_____ Ah_____

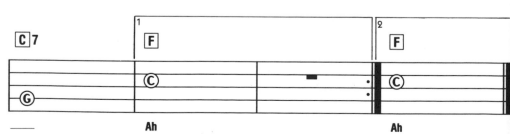

C 7 | 1 **F** | 2 **F**

_____ Ah Ah

Honky Cat

Regi-Sound Program: 8
Rhythm: Rock or Jazz Rock

Words and Music by
Elton John and Taupin

When I look back, boy, I must have been green,____

bop-pin' in the coun-try, fish-in' in a stream.____

Look-in' for an an-swer, try-in' to find a sign,____

un-til I saw your cit-y lights, hon-ey I was blind. They said,

get back, Honk-y Cat, bet-ter get back to the

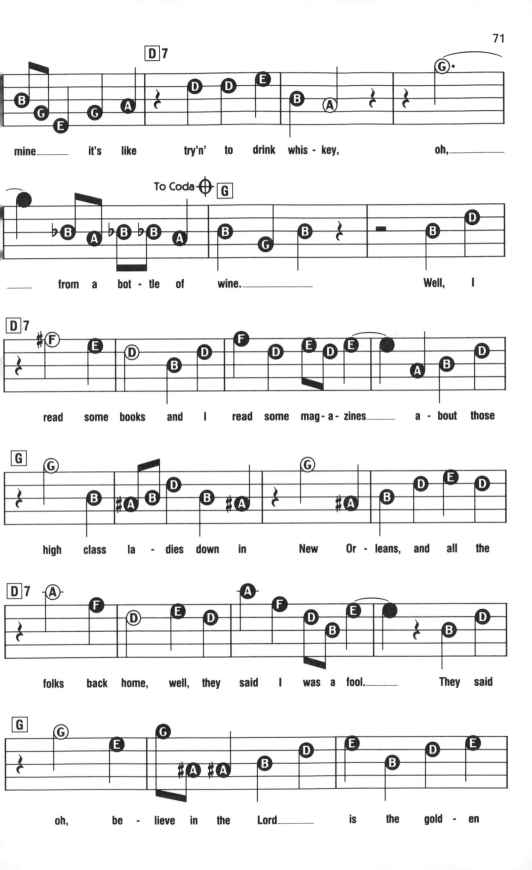

mine____ it's like try'n' to drink whis-key, oh,____

____ from a bot-tle of wine.____ Well, I

read some books and I read some mag-a-zines____ a-bout those

high class la-dies down in New Or-leans, and all the

folks back home, well, they said I was a fool.____ They said

oh, be-lieve in the Lord____ is the gold-en

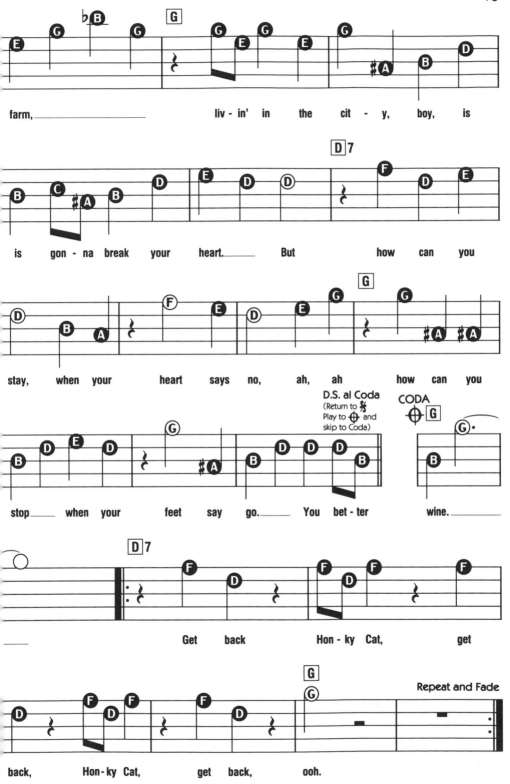

Grow Some Funk Of Your Own

Regi-Sound Program: 7
Rhythm: Rock

Words and Music by Elton John
Taupin and Davey Johnstone

Well I looked at my watch and it said
dreamed I'd been in a
looked for sup - port from the

quar - ter to five the head - lines screamed that I was
bor - der town. In a lit - tle can - tina that the
rest of my friends for their van - ishing trick they

still a - live. I could - n't un - der - stand it, I
boys had found. I was des - p'rate to dance Just to dig
set ten out of ten: I knelt to pray just to see

thought I died last night. Oh, I
the lo - cal sounds:
if he would compre -

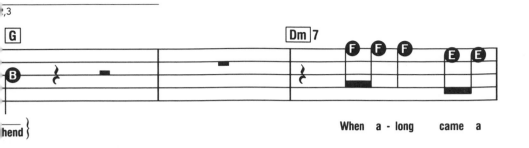

hend When a - long came a

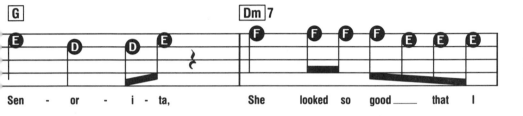

Sen - or - i - ta, She looked so good____ that I

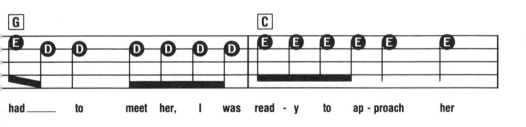

had____ to meet her, I was read - y to ap - proach her

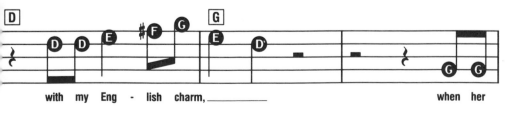

with my Eng - lish charm, _____ when her

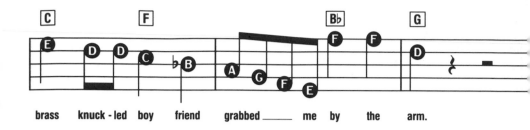

brass   knuck - led   boy   friend   grabbed ____ me   by   the   arm.

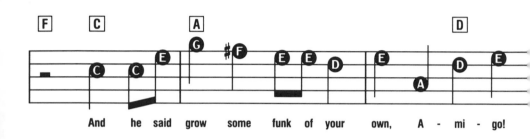

And   he   said   grow   some   funk   of   your   own,   A - mi - go!

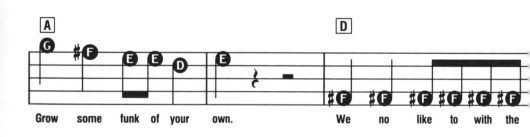

Grow   some   funk   of   your   own.   We   no   like   to   with   the

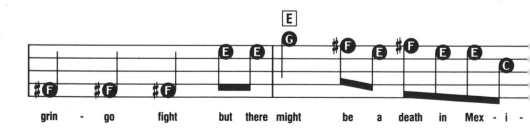

grin - go   fight   but   there   might   be   a   death   in   Mex - i -

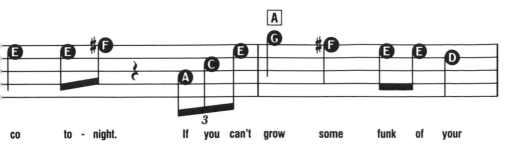

co to - night. If you can't grow some funk of your

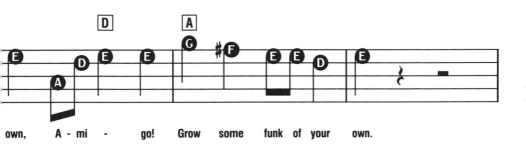

own, A - mi - go! Grow some funk of your own.

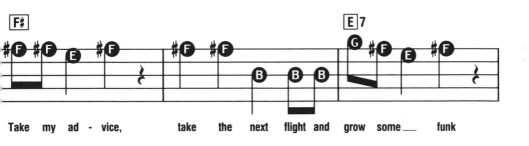

Take my ad - vice, take the next flight and grow some funk

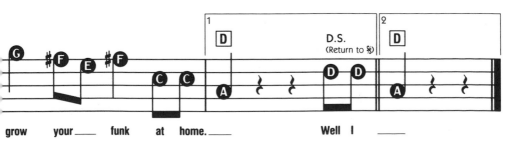

grow your funk at home. Well I

Healing Hands

Regi-Sound Program: 2
Rhythm: Rock or 8 Beat

Words and Music by
Elton John and Taupin

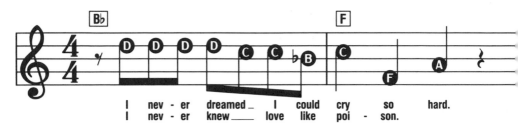

I nev - er dreamed __ I could cry so hard.
I nev - er knew __ love like poi - son.

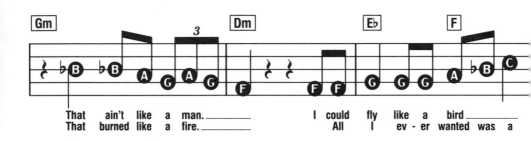

That ain't like a man. __
That burned like a fire. __

I could fly like a bird __
All I ev - er wanted was a

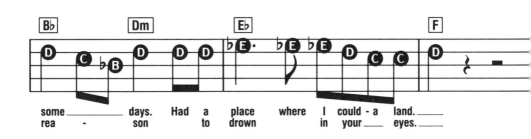

some __ days. Had a place where I could - a land. __
rea - son to drown in your __ eyes. __

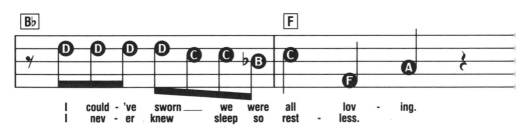

I could - 've sworn __ we were all lov - ing.
I nev - er knew sleep so rest - less.

Hm, ain't that what you say? _____ I nev - er
Hm, emp - ty arms _____ so cold. _____

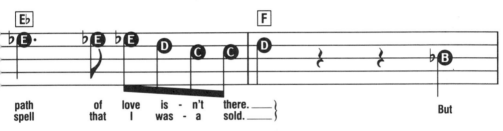

knew it could hurt_____ so_____ bad when the
That's not the way it's sup - posed _____ to be. It ain't the

path of love is - n't there. ___}
spell that I was - a sold. ___}

But

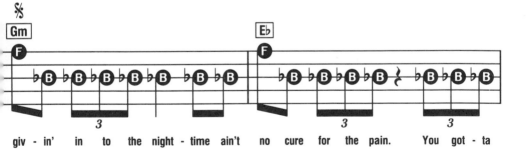

giv - in' in to the night - time ain't no cure for the pain. You got - ta

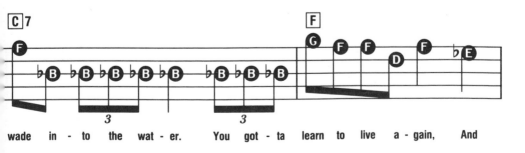

wade in - to the wat - er. You got - ta learn to live a - gain, And

I Don't Wanna Go On With You Like That

Regi-Sound Program: 5
Rhythm: Rock

Words and Music by
Elton John and Taupin

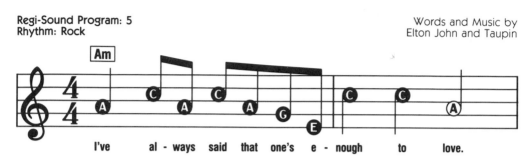

I've al - ways said that one's e - nough to love.

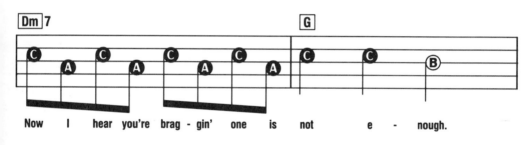

Now I hear you're brag - gin' one is not e - nough.

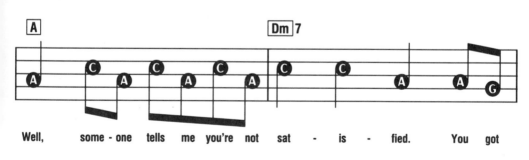

Well, some - one tells me you're not sat - is - fied. You got

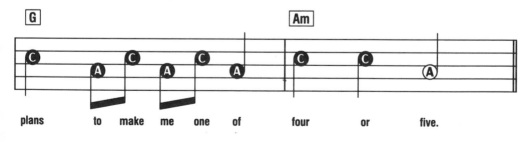

plans to make me one of four or five.

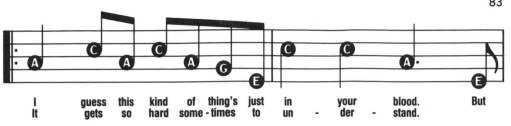

I guess this kind of thing's just in your blood. But
It gets so hard some-times to un - der - stand.

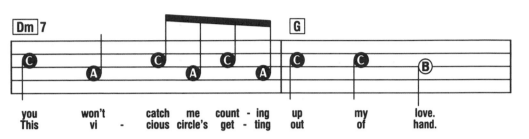

you won't catch me count - ing up my love.
This vi - cious circle's get - ting out of hand.

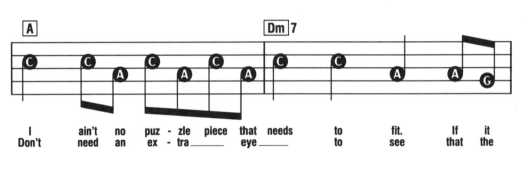

I ain't no puz - zle piece that needs to fit. If it
Don't need an ex - tra___ eye___ to see that the

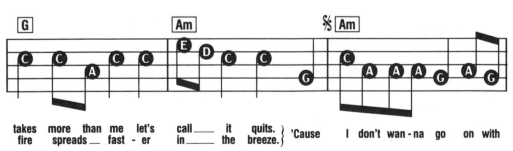

takes more than me let's call___ it quits.
fire spreads___ fast - er in___ the breeze. } 'Cause I don't wan - na go on with

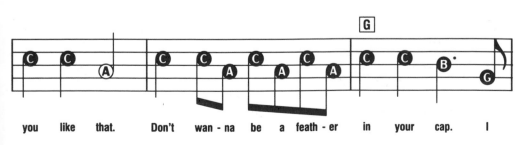

you like that. Don't wan - na be a feath - er in your cap. I

84

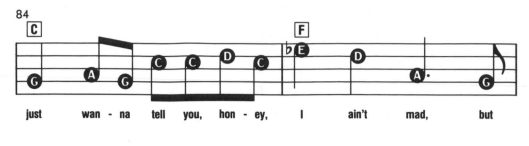

just wan - na tell you, hon - ey, I ain't mad, but

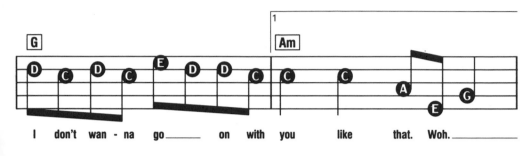

I don't wan - na go on with you like that. Woh.

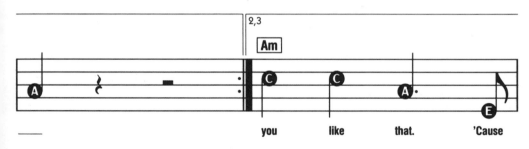

you like that. 'Cause

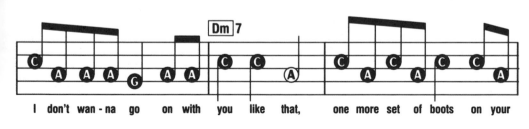

I don't wan - na go on with you like that, one more set of boots on your

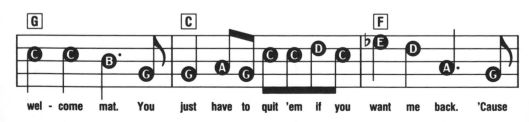

wel - come mat. You just have to quit 'em if you want me back. 'Cause

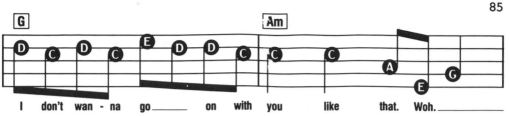

I don't wan - na go____ on with you like that. Woh.____

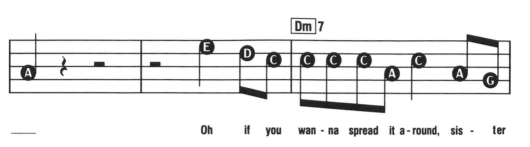

____ Oh if you wan - na spread it a - round, sis - ter

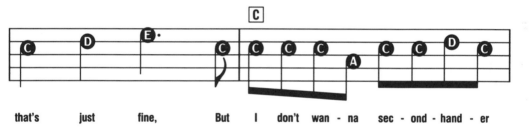

that's just fine, But I don't wan - na sec - ond - hand - er

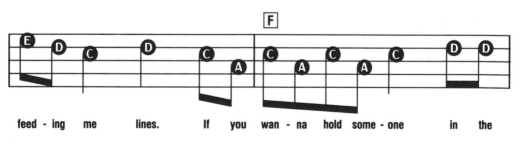

feed - ing me lines. If you wan - na hold some - one in the

D.S. and Fade
(Return to 𝄋 and fade)

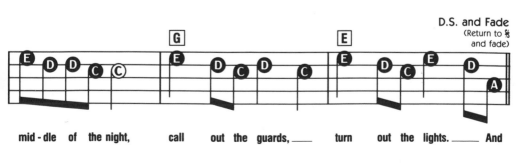

mid - dle of the night, call out the guards, ____ turn out the lights. ____ And

I Guess That's Why They Call It The Blues

Regi-Sound Program: 4
Rhythm: Ballad

Words and Music by Elton John,
Taupin and Davey Johnstone

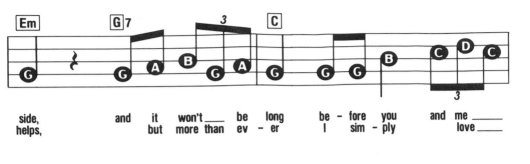

side, and it won't ___ be long be - fore you and me ___
helps, but more than ev - er I sim - ply love ___

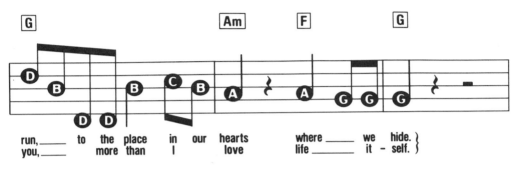

run, ___ to the place in our hearts where ___ we hide. ⎬
you, ___ more than I love life ___ it - self. ⎬

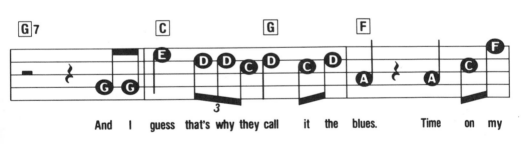

And I guess that's why they call it the blues. Time on my

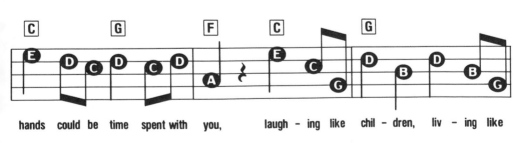

hands could be time spent with you, laugh - ing like chil - dren, liv - ing like

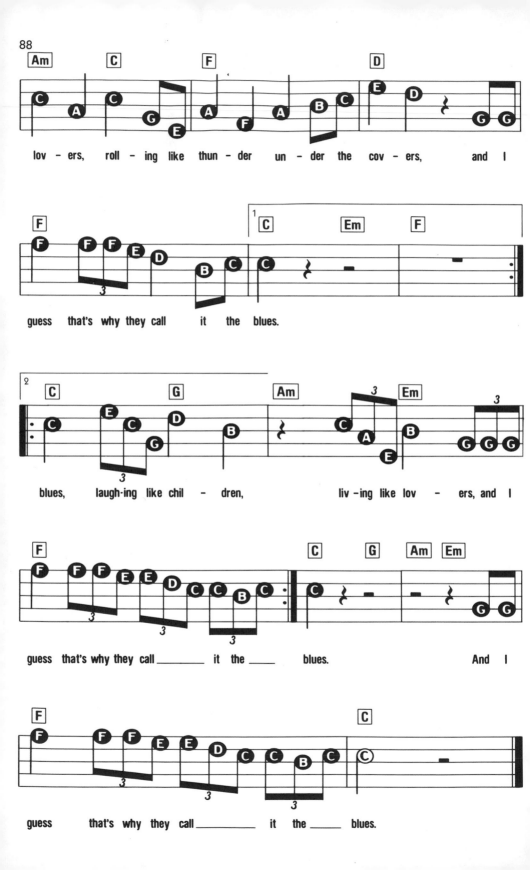

Island Girl

Regi-Sound Program: 7
Rhythm: Latin or Rhumba

Words and Music by
Elton John and Taupin

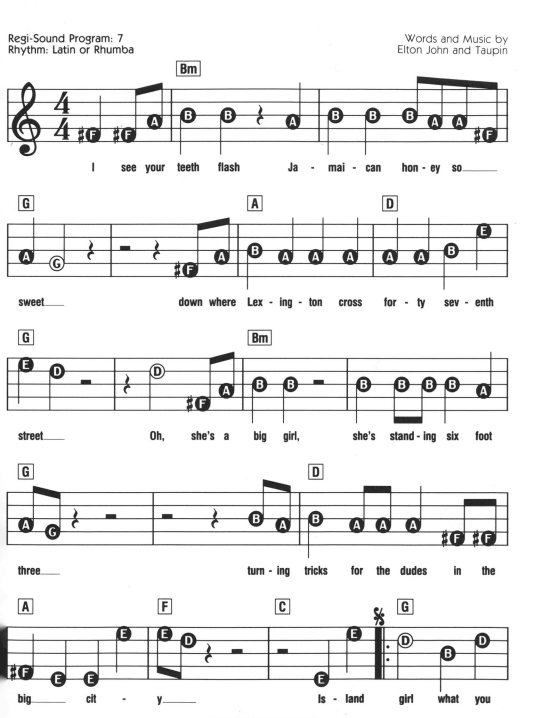

I'm Still Standing

Regi-Sound Program: 5
Rhythm: Rock or Jazz Rock

Words and Music by
Elton John and Taupin

1. You could nev - er know what it's like your
2. Did you think this fool could nev - er win Well,
3. *(see additional lyrics)*

blood like win - ter free - zes just like ice and there's a
look at me I'm com - in' back a - gain I got a

cold lone - ly light that shines from you you'll wind up like the wreck you
taste of love in a sim - ple way and if you need to know while I'm still

hide be - hind that mask you use.
stand - in', you just face a - way.

Don't you know,

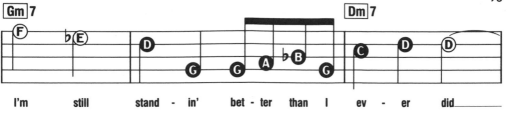

I'm still stand - in' bet - ter than I ev - er did

look - in' like a true sur - vi - vor, feel - in' like a

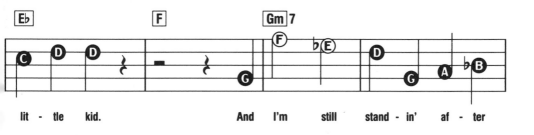

lit - tle kid. And I'm still stand - in' af - ter

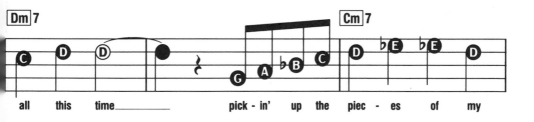

all this time pick - in' up the piec - es of my

life with - out you on my mind. I'm still stand - in',

94

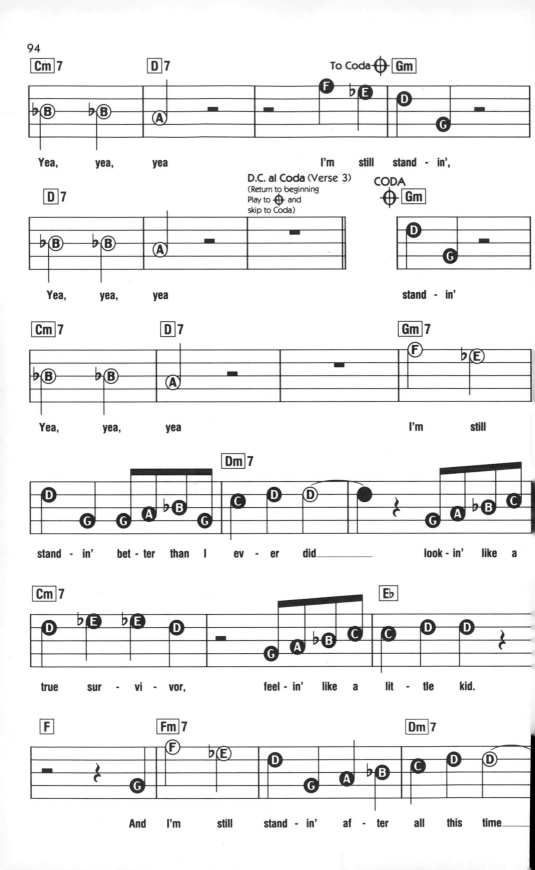

pick - in' up the piec - es of my life with - out you

on my mind. I'm still stand - in',

Yea, yea, yea I'm still

stand - in', Yea, yea, yea I'm still

Repeat and Fade

Verse 3
Once I never could hope to win
You starting down the road
Leaving me again, The threats
you made were meant to cut me down
And if our love was just a circus
You'd be a clown by now.

Kiss The Bride

Regi-Sound Program: 4
Rhythm: Rock

Words and Music by
Elton John and Taupin

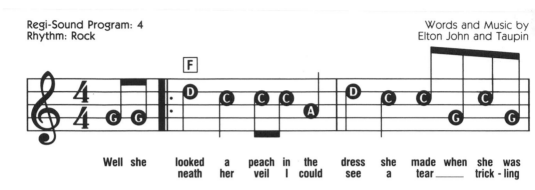

Well she looked a peach in the dress she made when she was
neath her veil I could see a tear_____ trick-ling

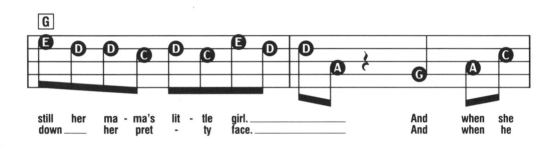

still her ma-ma's lit-tle girl._____ And when she
down_____ her pret-ty face._____ And when he

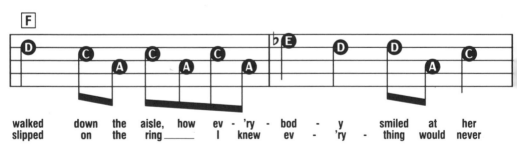

walked down the aisle, how ev-'ry-bod-y smiled at her
slipped on the ring_____ I knew ev-'ry-thing would never

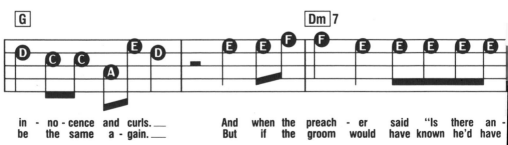

in-no-cence and curls. ___ And when the preach-er said "Is there an-
be the same a-gain. ___ But if the groom would have known he'd have

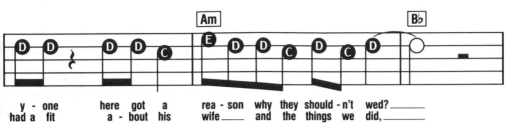

y - one   here   got   a   rea - son   why   they   should - n't   wed?_____
had a   fit   a - bout   his   wife_____   and   the   things   we   did, _____

I   should   have   stuck   up   my   hand.   I   should   have   got   up   to
And   what   I   planned _ to   say.   Yeah   on   her   wed - ding_____

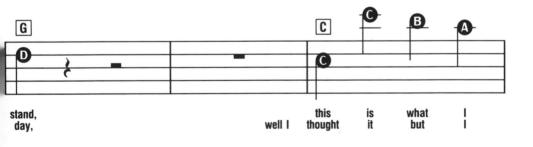

stand,   this   is   what   I
day,   well I   thought   it   but   I

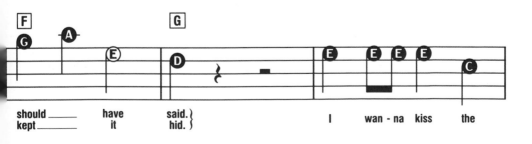

should _____ have   said.   I   wan - na   kiss   the
kept _____ it   hid.

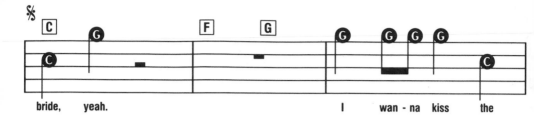

bride,   yeah.   I   wan - na   kiss   the

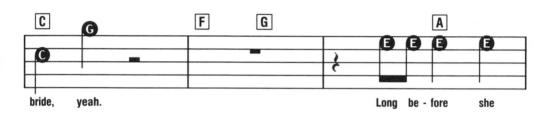

bride,   yeah.   Long   be - fore   she

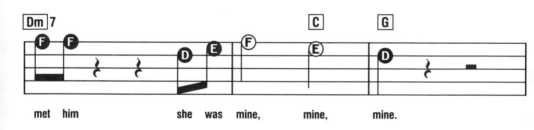

met   him   she   was   mine,   mine,   mine.

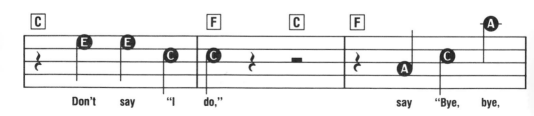

Don't   say   "I   do,"   say   "Bye,   bye,

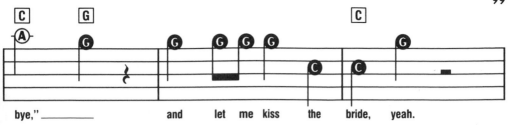

bye," _____ and let me kiss the bride, yeah.

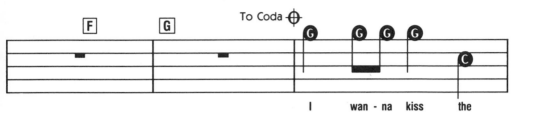

To Coda

I wan - na kiss the

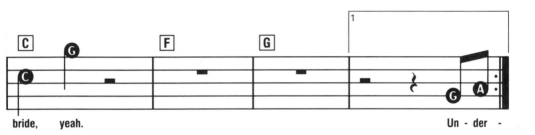

bride, yeah. Un - der -

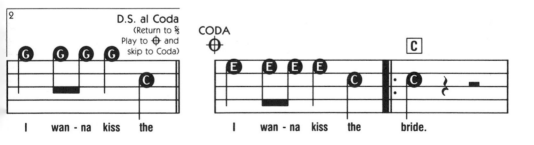

D.S. al Coda
(Return to %
Play to ⊕ and
skip to Coda)

CODA

I wan - na kiss the

I wan - na kiss the bride.

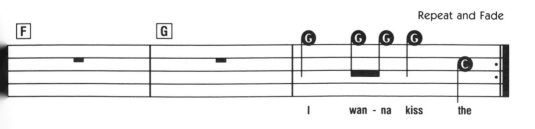

Repeat and Fade

I wan - na kiss the

Levon

Regi-Sound Program: 1
Rhythm: Ballad

Words and Music by
Elton John and Taupin

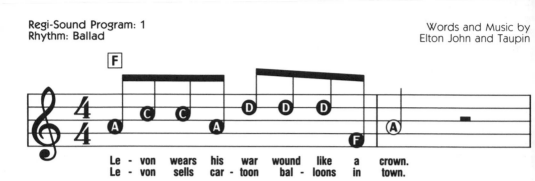

Le - von wears his war wound like a crown.
Le - von sells car - toon bal - loons in town.

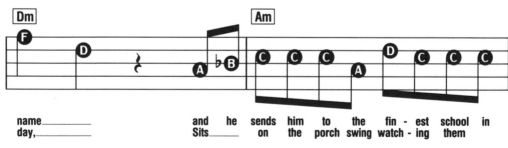

He calls his child_____ Je - sus_____ 'cause he likes the
His fam - 'ly bus - 'ness thrives_____ Jesus blows up bal- loons all

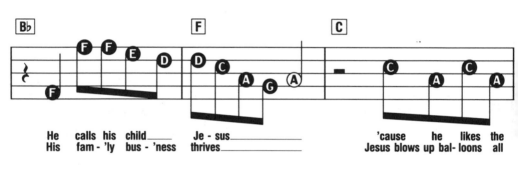

name_____ and he sends him to the fin - est school in
day,_____ Sits_____ on the porch swing watch - ing them

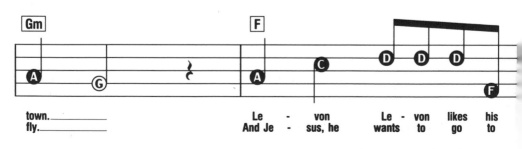

town._____ Le - von Le - von likes his
fly._____ And Je - sus, he wants to go to

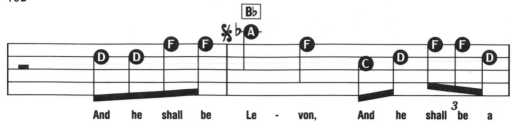

And he shall be Le - von, And he shall be a

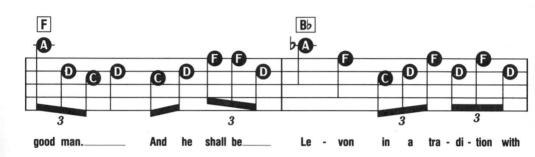

good man._____ And he shall be_____ Le - von in a tra - di - tion with

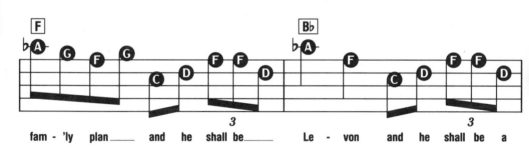

fam - 'ly plan_____ and he shall be_____ Le - von and he shall be a

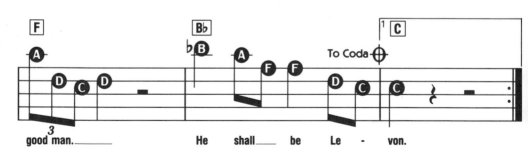

good man._____ He shall____ be Le - von.

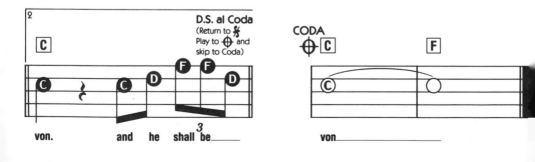

von.   and he shall be_____   von_____

Lucy In The Sky With Diamonds

Regi-Sound Program: 8
Rhythm: Waltz

Words and Music by
John Lennon and Paul McCartney

Pic - ture your - self in a boat on a
Fol - low her down to a bridge by a
Pic - ture your - self on a train in a

riv - er with tan - ger - ine trees and mar - ma - lade
foun - tain where rock - ing horse peo - ple eat marsh - mal - low
sta - tion with plas - ti - cine port - ers with look - ing glass

skies. Some - bod - y calls you, you
pies. Ev' - ry - one smiles as you
ties. Sud - en - ly some - one is

an - swer quite slow - ly a girl with kal - eid - o - scope
drift past the flow - ers that grow so in - cred - i - bly
there at the turn - stile the girl with kal - eid - o - scope

eyes.
high.
eyes.

Cel - lo - phane flow - ers of yel - low and green
News - pa - per tax - is ap - pear on the shore

tow - er - ing o - ver your head.
wait - ing to take you a - way.

Look for the girl with the sun in her eyes and she's
Climb in the back with your head in the clouds and you're

Rhythm: Rock

gone.
gone.

Lu - cy in the sky ____ with dia - monds,

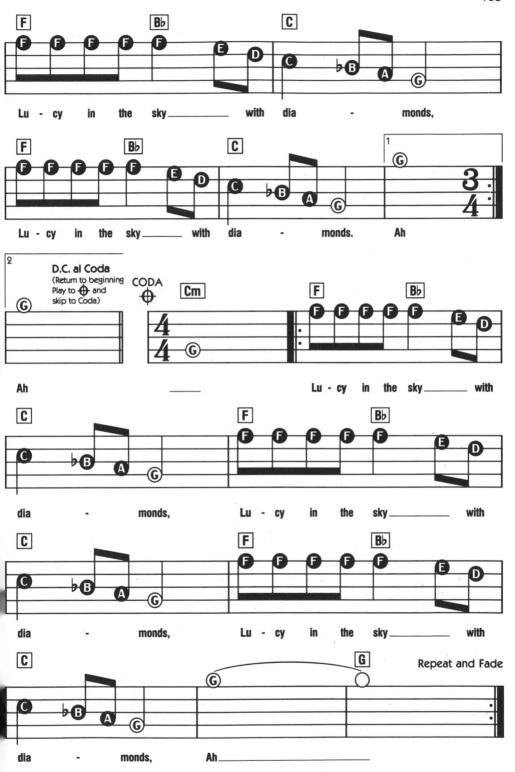

Little Jeannie

Regi-Sound Program: 4
Rhythm: Latin or Bossa Nova

Words and Music by
Elton John and Gary Osborne

Oh, lit - tle Jean - nie, you got
Lit - tle Jean - nie, you got

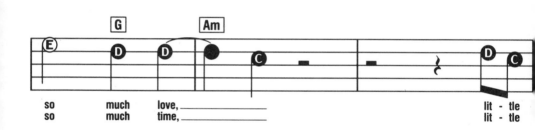

so much love, _____ lit - tle
so much time, _____ lit - tle

Jean - nie. And you take it where it
Jean - nie. Though you've grown be - yond your

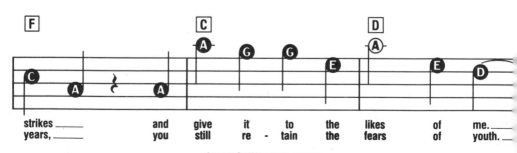

strikes _____ and give it to the likes of me.
years, _____ you still re - tain the fears of youth. _____

(third time instrumental)

want you to be my ac - ro - bat. I

want you to be my lov -er._____

Oh, there were
Oh, there were
Oh, there were

oth - ers who would treat you cruel._____
oth - ers who would treat you cruel._____
oth - ers, and I've known quite a few._____

To Coda

And oh,_____ Jean - nie,
But oh,_____ Jean - nie,
But oh,_____ Jean - nie,

you were al - ways some - one's ___ fool. I will

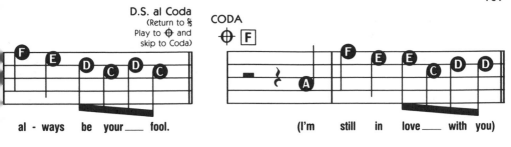

al - ways be your___ fool. (I'm still in love___ with you)

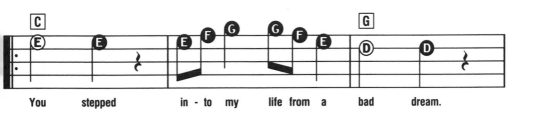

You stepped in - to my life from a bad dream.

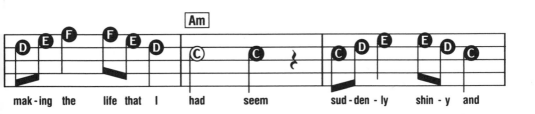

mak - ing the life that I had seem sud - den - ly shin - y and

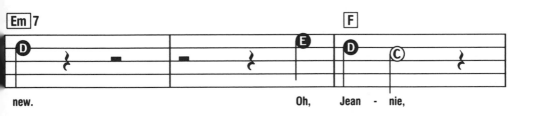

new. Oh, Jean - nie,

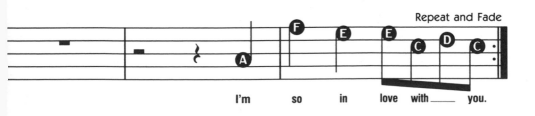

I'm so in love with___ you.

Madman Across The Water

Regi-Sound Program: 8
Rhythm: Rock

Words and Music by
Elton John and Taupin

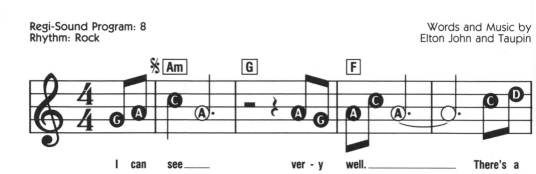

I can see_____ ver - y well._____ There's a

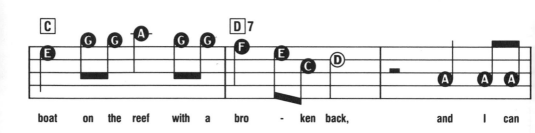

boat on the reef with a bro - ken back, and I can

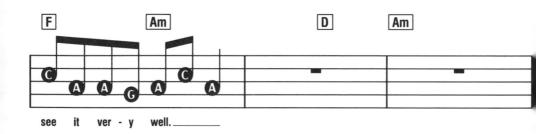

see it ver - y well._____

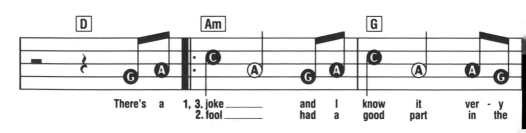

There's a   1, 3. joke_____   and I know it ver - y
   2. fool_____   had a good part in the

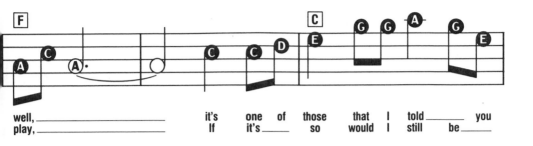

well,_____ it's one of those that I told_____ you
play,_____ If it's_____ so would I still be_____

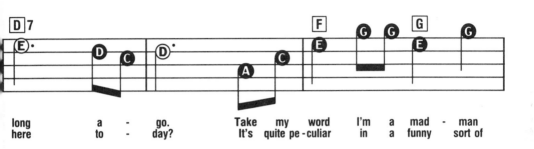

long a - go. Take my word I'm a mad - man
here to - day? It's quite pe - culiar in a funny sort of

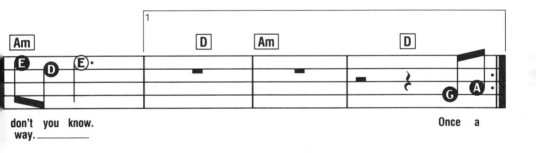

don't you know. Once a
way._____

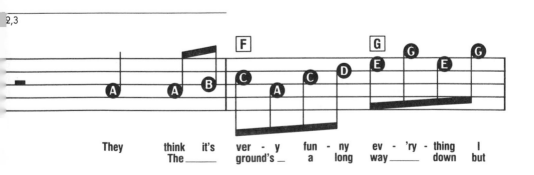

They think it's ver - y fun - ny ev - 'ry - thing I
The_____ ground's _ a long way_____ down but

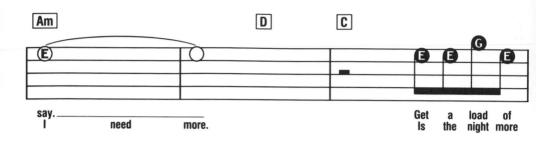

say. I need more.
Get a load of
Is the night more

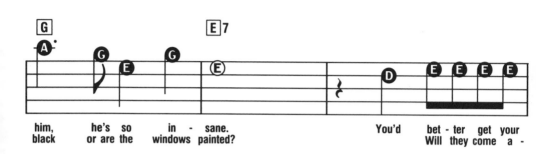

him, he's so in - sane.
black or are the windows painted?
You'd bet - ter get your
Will they come a -

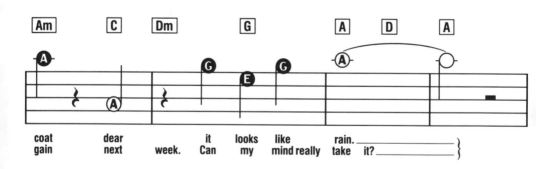

coat dear it looks like rain.
gain next week. Can my mind really take it?

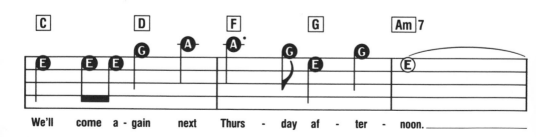

We'll come a - gain next Thurs - day af - ter - noon.

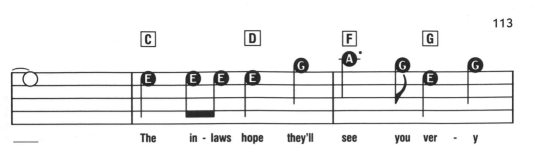

The in - laws hope they'll see you ver - y

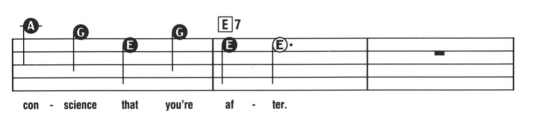

soon. _____ But is it in your

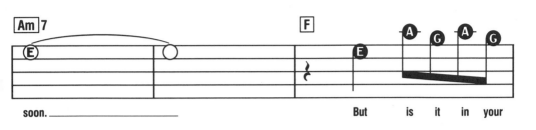

con - science that you're af - ter.

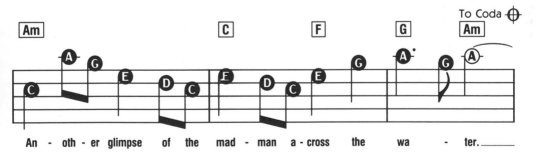

An - oth - er glimpse of the mad - man a - cross the wa - ter. ___

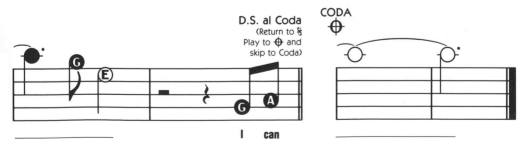

D.S. al Coda
(Return to %
Play to ⊕ and
skip to Coda)

CODA
⊕

I can

Madness

Regi-Sound Program: 5
Rhythm: Rock

Words and Music by
Elton John and Gary Osborne

1. The fuse is set and checked once more.
2. hide in - side a smoke - filled room.
3, 4. (See additional lyrics)

Then left be - side a
To hear at last the

back street door._____ And in the cold__
blast of doom._____ And so the deed__

_____ grey light. They Some - one sees a
_____ is done. They lis - ten to the

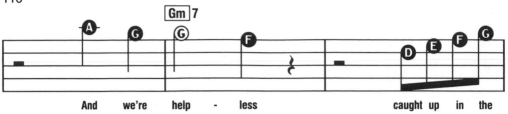

And we're help - less caught up in the

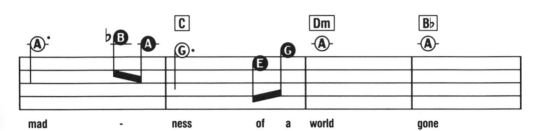

mad - ness of a world gone

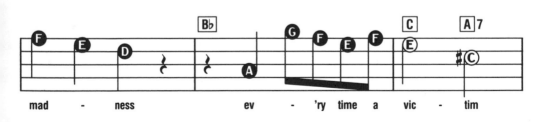

mad,_____ The And it's

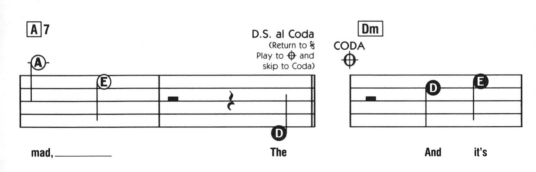

mad - ness ev - 'ry time a vic - tim

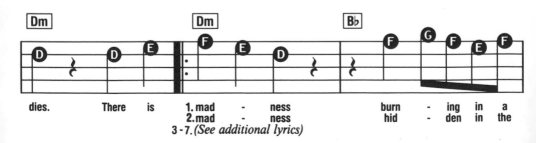

dies. There is 1. mad - ness burn - ing in a
2. mad - ness hid - den in the
3 - 7. *(See additional lyrics)*

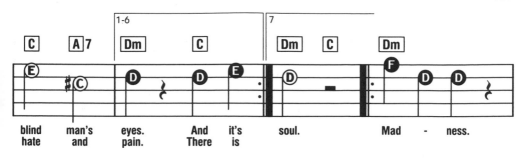

| blind | man's | eyes. | And | it's | soul. | Mad | - | ness. |
| hate | and | pain. | There | is | | | | |

Repeat and Fade

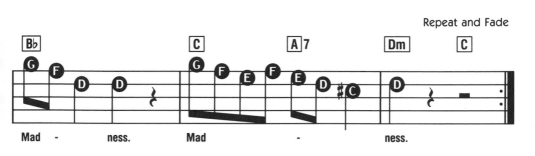

| Mad | - | ness. | Mad | - | ness. |

Additional Lyrics

Verse
3. The roar of fire rings out on high.
And flames light up the black night sky.
A child screams out in fear.
A helpless cry for help but no one is near to hear.

4. As walls collapse and timbers flare,
The smell of death hangs in the air.
When help at last arrives,
They try to fight the flames but nothing survives of all those lives.

Coda
3. Madness, burning in a wild man's brain. And it's
4. Madness, everytime the bullets start. There is
5. Madness, burning in a poor man's heart. And it's
6. Madness, something that we can't control. There is
7. Madness, burning in a blind man's soul.

Michelle's Song

(From the motion picture "FRIENDS")

Regi-Sound Program: 7
Rhythm: Rock

Words and Music by
Elton John and Taupin

Cast a peb - ble on the wa - ter, watch the
Sleep - ing in the o - pen, see the
learned to be so grace - ful, watch - ing

rip - ples gent - ly spread - ing, ti - ny daugh - ter of the
shad - ows soft - ly mov - ing, take a train to - wards the
wild hors - es run - ning and from those a - gile

Cam - argue, we were meant to be to - geth - er.
south - land, our time was nev - er bet - ter.
an - gels, we knew the tide was turn - ing.

We were made for one an - oth - er in a
We shall pass the sights of splen - dor on the
For we watched as on the sky - way the

119

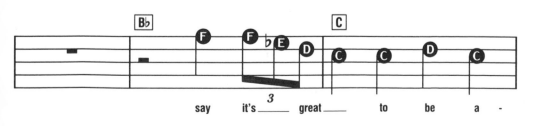

Mona Lisa and Mad Hatters
(Part Two)

Regi-Sound Program: 5
Rhythm: Rock

Words and Music by
Elton John and Taupin

I used to think that New York Cit - y
I heard a bas - ket - ball

fell from grace with God, and in - no-cence a -
some - where out be-yond a chain - link fence. In - ner cit - y

broad waged a war for the un - der - dog.
prisoners ar - gue for the right of self - de - fense. But

When the snow - falls and Cen - tral Park looks like a Christ - mas
there's a fast break, and ev - 'ry work of art wakes some - thing in the

card. / soul.

I just looked be - yond the bag - man and the / Just fo - cus on the___ brush - strokes and the

mad - ness that makes this cit - y hard. } / bou - quets___ that the danc - ers hold. }

Span - ish Har - lem still sounds good to _____ me.

Yeah, Mo - na Li - sa's get - ting old - er.

Stand - ing in the shad - ow of Miss Lib - er - ty. While I

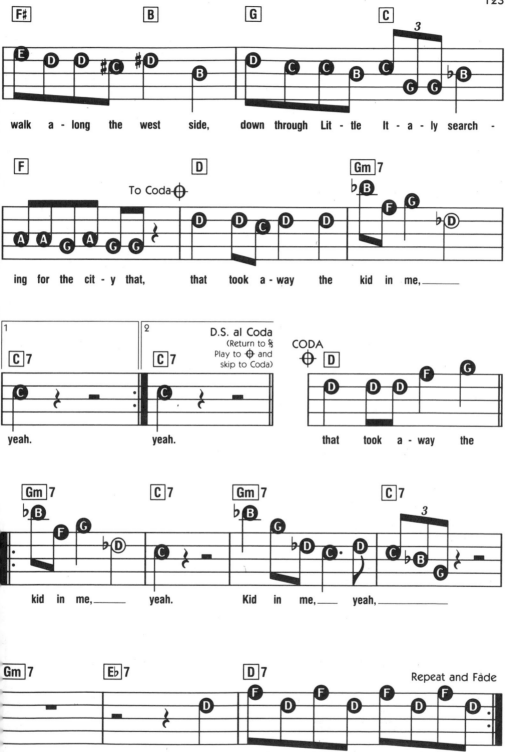

123

Nikita

Regi-Sound Program: 3
Rhythm: Slow Rock or Rock

Words and Music by
Elton John and Taupin

125

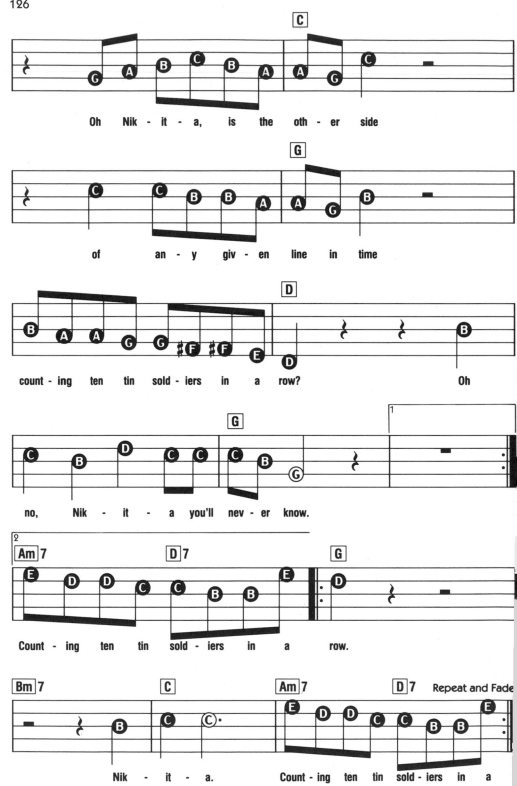

Sartorial Eloquence

Regi-Sound Program: 7
Rhythm: Rock

Words and Music by
Elton John and Tom Robinson

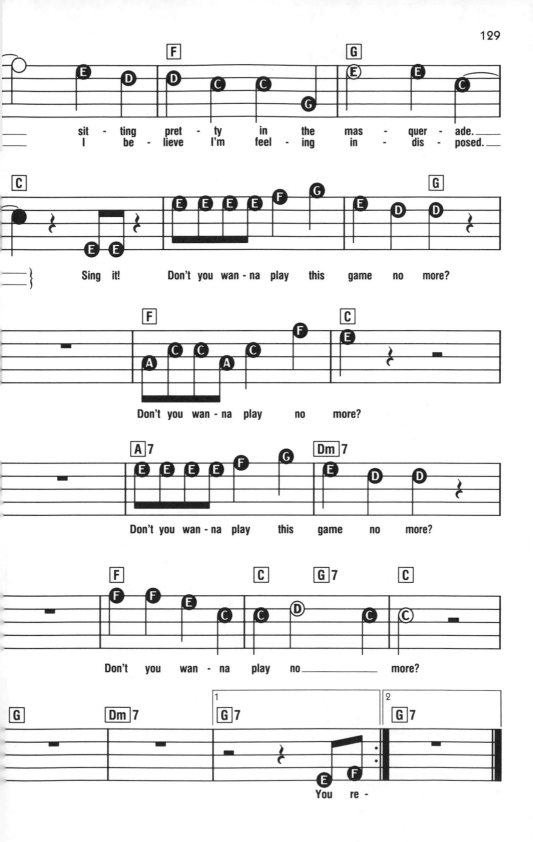

Nobody Wins

Regi-Sound Program: 7
Rhythm: Rock

French Words and Music by Jean-Paul Dreau
English Words by Gary Osborne

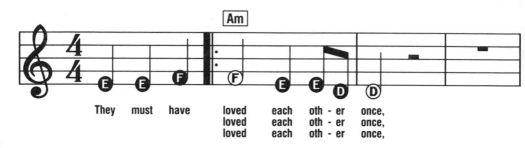

They must have loved each oth - er once,
loved each oth - er once,
loved each oth - er once,

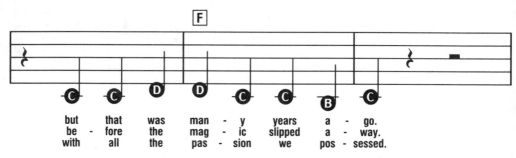

but that was man - y years a - go.
be - fore the mag - ic slipped a - way.
with all the pas - sion we pos - sessed.

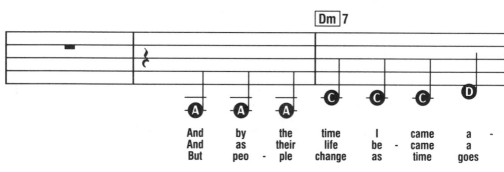

And by the time I came a -
And as their life be - came a
But peo - ple change as time goes

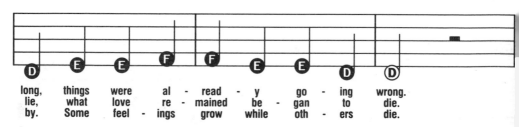

long, things were al - read - y go - ing wrong.
lie, what love re - mained be - gan to die.
by. Some feel - ings grow while oth - ers die.

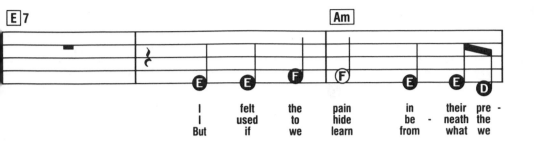

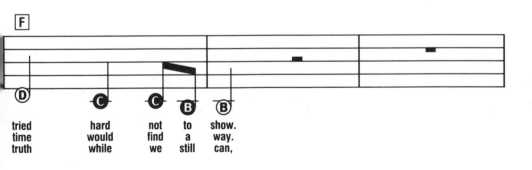

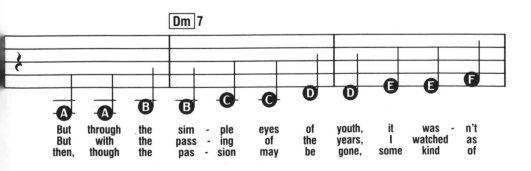

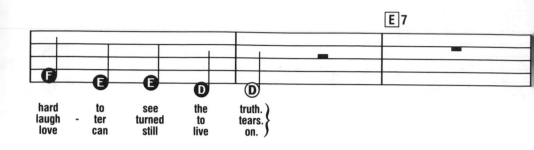

hard	to	see	the	truth.
laugh	- ter	turned	to	tears.
love	can	still	live	on.

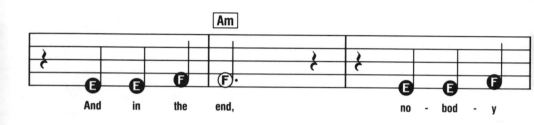

And in the end, no - bod - y

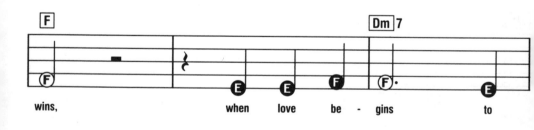

wins, when love be - gins to

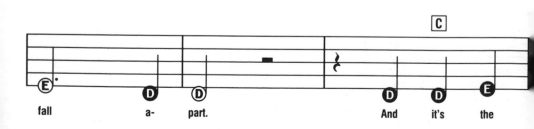

fall a- part. And it's the

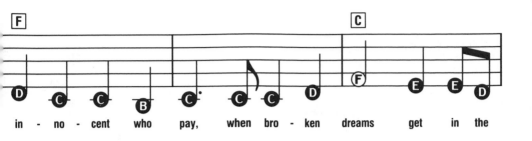

in - no - cent who pay, when bro - ken dreams get in the

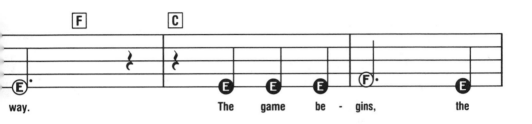

way. The game be - gins, the

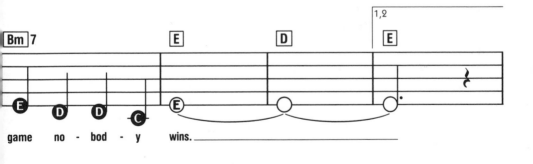

game no - bod - y wins.

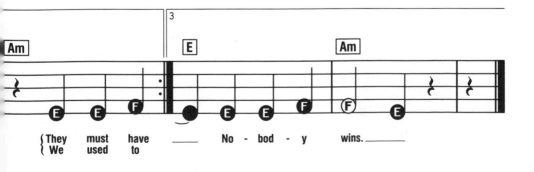

{ They must have _____ No - bod - y wins. _____
{ We used to

Philadelphia Freedom

Regi-Sound Program: 7
Rhythm: Rock

Words and Music by
Elton John and Taupin

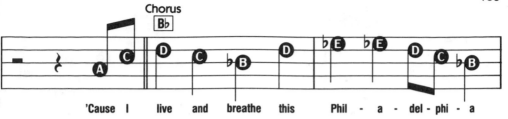

Chorus

'Cause I live and breathe this Phil - a - del - phi - a

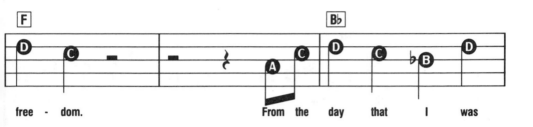

free - dom. From the day that I was

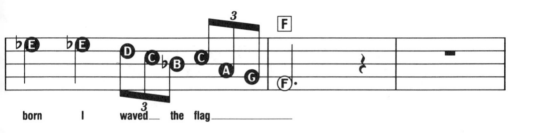

born I waved the flag

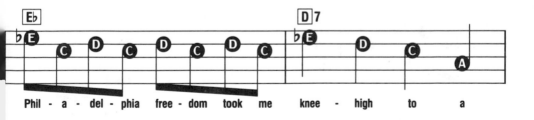

Phil - a - del - phia free - dom took me knee - high to a

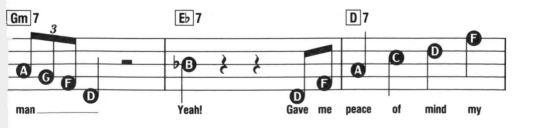

man Yeah! Gave me peace of mind my

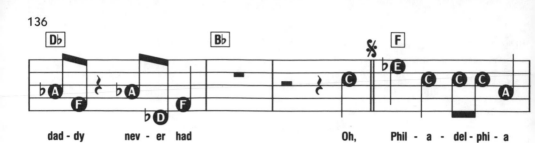

dad - dy   nev - er had   Oh,   Phil - a - del - phi - a

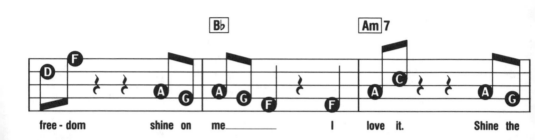

free - dom   shine on   me_____   I   love it.   Shine the

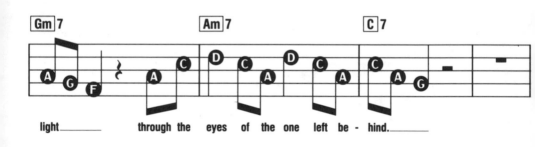

light_____   through the   eyes   of   the one   left be - hind._____

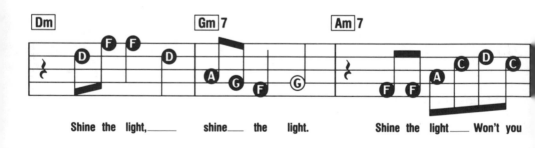

Shine the   light,_____   shine____ the   light.   Shine the light____ Won't you

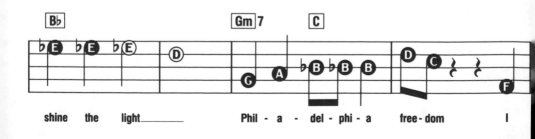

shine   the   light_____   Phil - a - del - phi - a   free - dom   I

2. If you choose to, you can live your life alone
Some people choose the city
Some others choose the good old family home
I like living easy without family ties
'Til the whippoorwill of freedom zapped me
Right between the eyes
(to Chorus)

Rocket Man
(I Think It's Gonna Be A Long Long Time)

Regi-Sound Program: 5
Rhythm: Ballad

Words and Music by
Elton John and Taupin

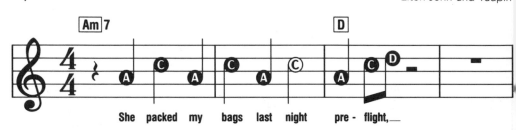

She packed my bags last night pre - flight, ___

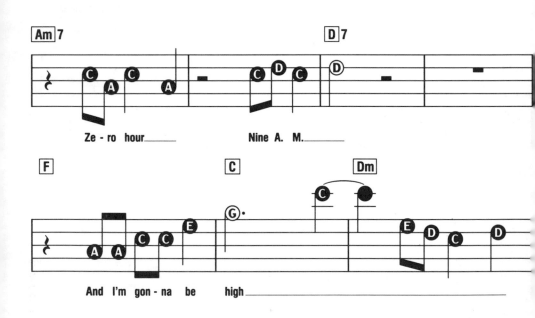

Ze - ro hour ___ Nine A. M. ___

And I'm gon - na be high ___

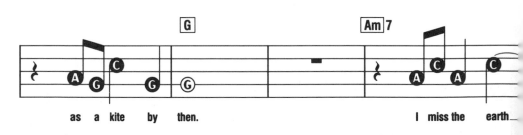

as a kite by then. I miss the earth ___

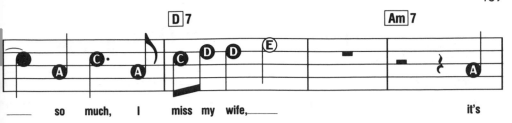

so much, I miss my wife,_____ it's

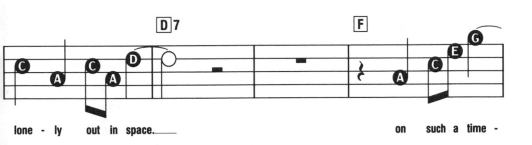

lone - ly out in space._____ on such a time -

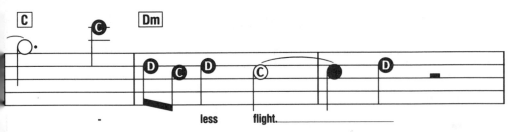

- less flight._____

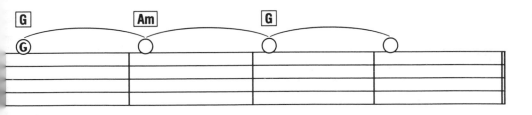

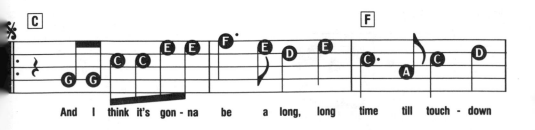

And I think it's gon - na be a long, long time till touch - down

brings me round a - gain to find I'm not the man they think I am at

home, Oh no no no, I'm a rock - et man.

Rock - et man burn - ing out his fuse up here a - lone.

To Coda

Mars ain't the kind of place to raise your kids,

In fact it's cold as hell.

Sad Songs
(Say So Much)

Regi-Sound Program: 6
Rhythm: Rock or Jazz Rock

Words and Music by
Elton John and Taupin

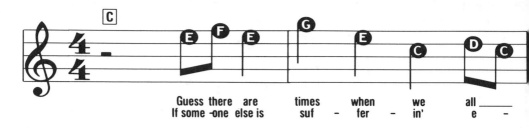

Guess there are   times   when   we   all _____
If some -one else is   suf - fer - in'   e -

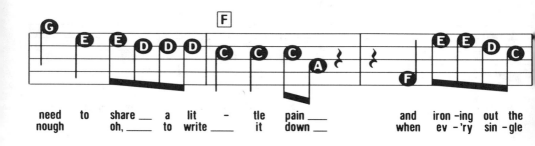

need   to   share ___ a   lit - tle   pain ___   and   iron -ing   out   the
nough   oh, _____ to   write _____   it   down ___   when   ev -'ry   sin -gle

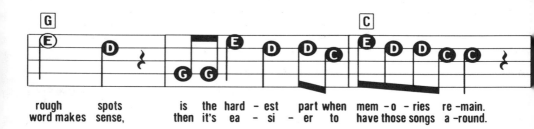

rough   spots   is   the   hard - est   part   when   mem -o - ries   re -main.
word   makes   sense,   then   it's   ea - si - er   to   have those songs   a -round.

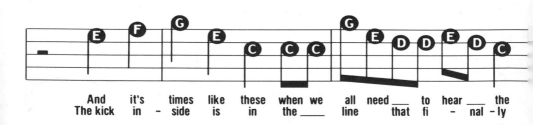

And   it's   times   like   these   when we   all   need ___ to   hear ___ the
The kick   in - side   is   in   the ___   line   that   fi - nal - ly

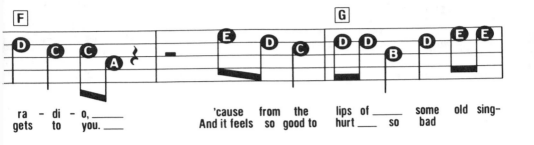

ra - di - o, _____ 'cause from the lips of ____ some old sing-
gets to you. ___ And it feels so good to hurt ___ so bad

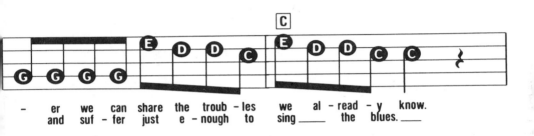

- er we can share the troub - les we al - read - y know.
and suf - fer just e - nough to sing ____ the blues. ___

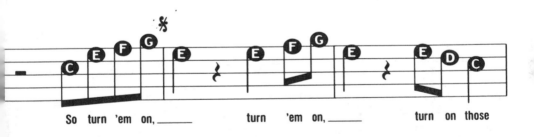

So turn 'em on, _____ turn 'em on, _____ turn on those

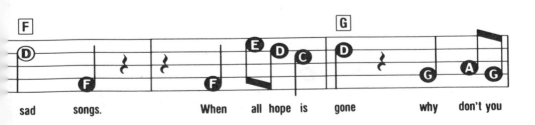

sad songs. When all hope is gone why don't you

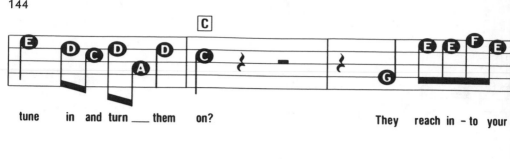

tune   in   and   turn ___ them   on?   They   reach   in – to   your

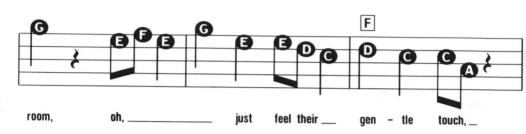

room,   oh, _____   just   feel   their ___ gen – tle   touch, __

To Coda ⊕

When   all   hope   is   gone   a   sad   song __ says __ so

much.   much.   Sad   songs, __ they __

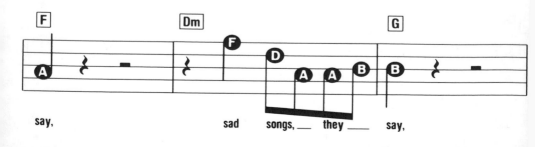

say,   sad   songs, __ they __ say,

145

sad   songs, __ they __ say,   sad   songs, __ they __

D.S. al Coda
(Return to 𝄋
Play to ⊕ and
skip to Coda)

CODA

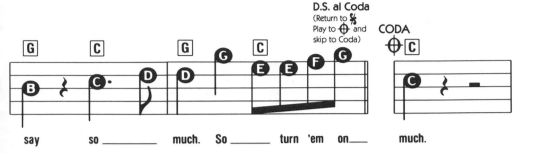

say   so _____ much. So _____ turn 'em on__ much.

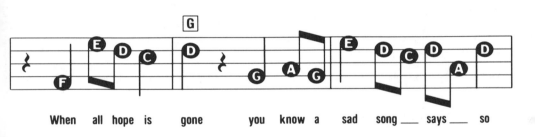

When   all hope is   gone   you know a sad song __ says __ so

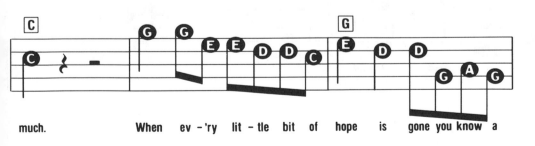

much.   When ev-'ry lit-tle bit of hope   is   gone you know a

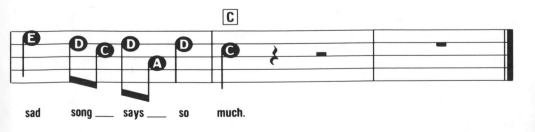

sad   song __ says __ so   much.

Saturday Night's Alright
(For Fighting)

Regi-Sound Program: 3
Rhythm: Rock or Jazz Rock

Words and Music by
Elton John and Taupin

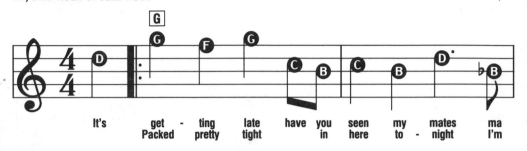

It's   get - ting   late   have you   seen   my   mates   ma
Packed   pretty   tight   in   here   to - night   I'm

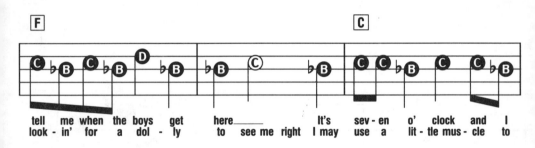

tell   me   when the boys   get   here_____   It's   sev - en   o' clock   and   I
look - in'   for   a   dol - ly   to   see me right   I may   use a   lit - tle mus - cle   to

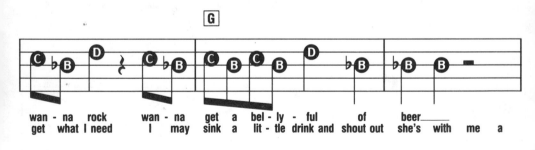

wan - na   rock   wan - na   get a   bel - ly - ful   of   beer_____
get   what I need   I   may   sink a   lit - tle drink and   shout out   she's   with   me   a

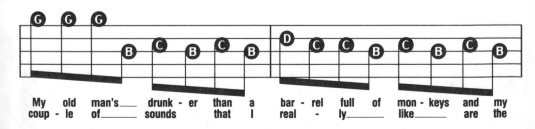

My   old   man's____   drunk - er   than   a   bar - rel   full   of   mon - keys   and   my
coup - le   of_____   sounds   that   I   real - ly____   like____   are   the

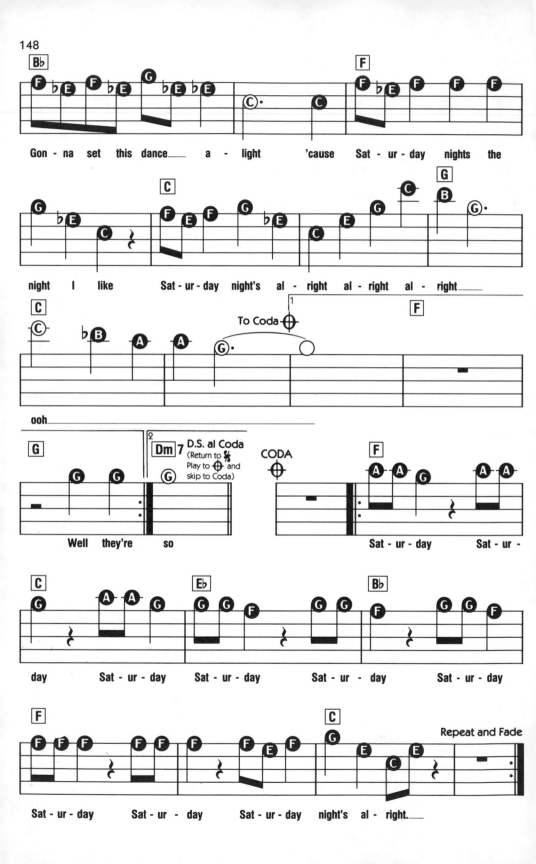

Song For Guy

Regi-Sound Program: 8
Rhythm: Latin

By Elton John

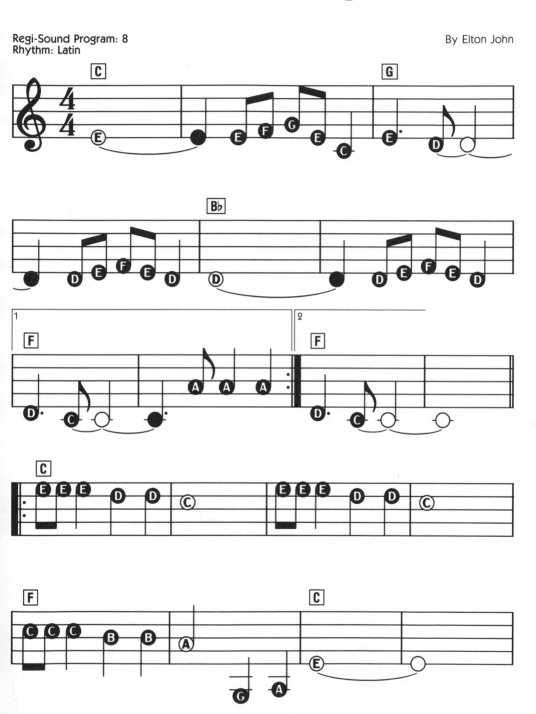

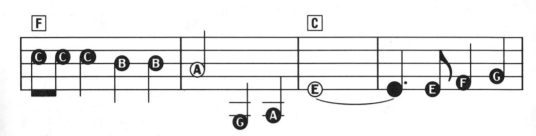

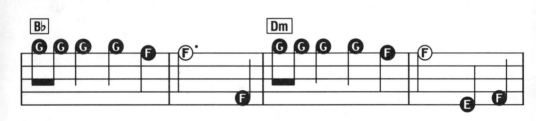

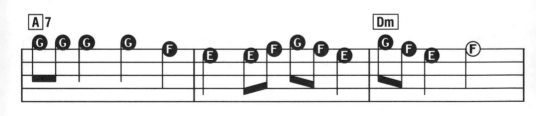

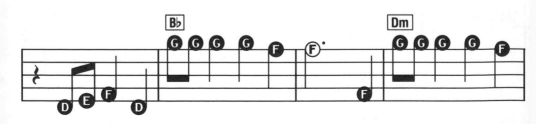

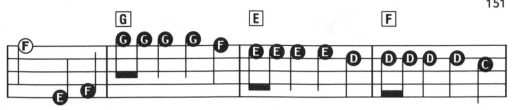

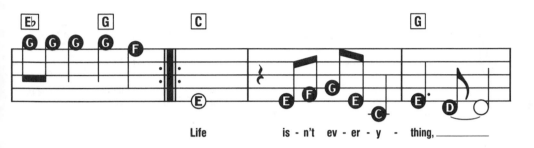

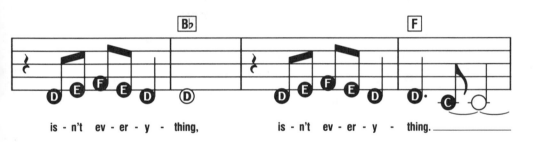

Life   is - n't ev - er - y - thing, _____

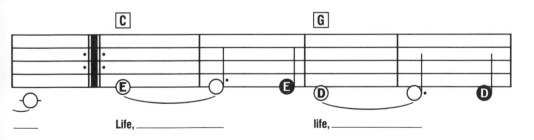

is - n't ev - er - y - thing,   is - n't ev - er - y - thing. _____

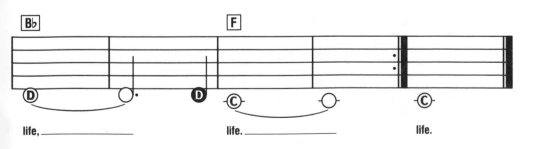

_____   Life, _____   life, _____

life, _____   life. _____   life.

Sixty Years On

Regi-Sound Program: 3
Rhythm: 8 Beat or Pops

Words and Music by
Elton John and Taupin

you,_____ my ro - sa - ry has bro - ken, and my
gun,_____ I've no wish to be liv - ing
you,_____ your chor - al lamp that burns so low when

beads_____ have all_____ slipped through.
six - ty_____ years_____ on.
you are_____ pass - ing

through,_____ and the fu - ture you're giv - ing me holds

noth - ing for a gun._____ I've no wish to be

liv - ing, six - ty years_____ on.

Skyline Pigeon

Regi-Sound Program: 4
Rhythm: 8 Beat or Pops

Words and Music by
Elton John and Taupin

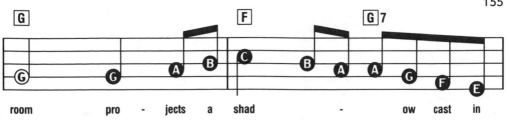

room pro - jects a shad - ow cast in

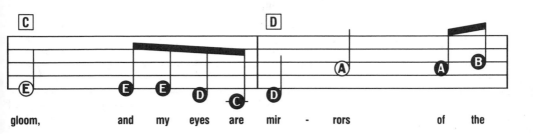

gloom, and my eyes are mir - rors of the

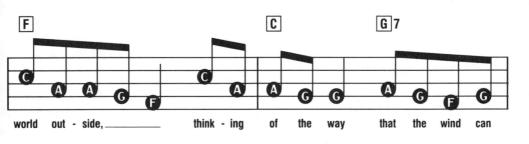

world out - side,_____ think - ing of the way that the wind can

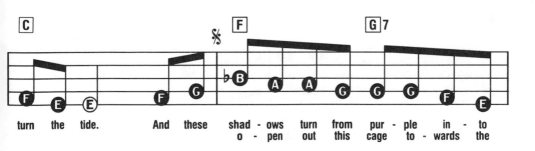

turn the tide. And these shad - ows turn from pur - ple in - to
o - pen out this cage to - wards the

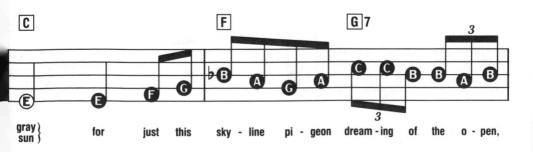

gray }
sun }
for just this sky - line pi - geon dream - ing of the o - pen,

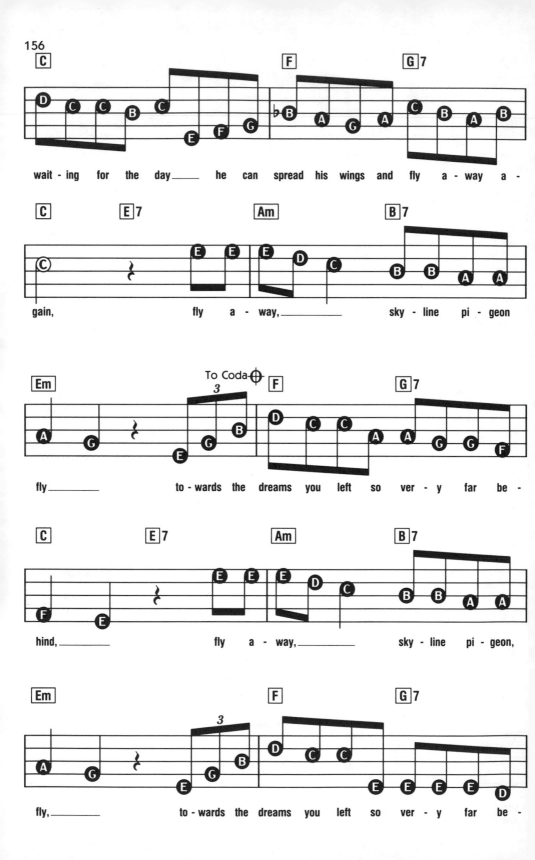

hind. _____ Just let me wake up in the morn - ing to the

smell of new - mown hay, to laugh and cry, to live and die ____ in the

bright - ness of my day, I wan - na hear the peal - ing bells of dis - tant

church - es sing, but most of all, please free me from this ach - ing

D.S. al Coda
(Return to %
Play to ⊕ and
skip to Coda)

CODA

met - al ring, and things you left so ver - y, so

ver - y far _____ be - hind. _____

Someone Saved My Life Tonight

Regi-Sound Program: 7
Rhythm: 8 Beat or Pops

Words and Music by
Elton John and Taupin

When I think of those east end lights,
I nev - er re - al - ized the pass -

mug - gy nights, the cur - tains drawn in the lit - tle room down - stairs
ing hours Of ev - en - ing show - ers, a slip noose hang -

Prim - a don - na, lord you real - ly should have been there,
ing in my dark - est dreams. I'm stran - gled by your

sit - ting like a prin - cess perched in her e - lec - tric chair. And it's
haunt - ed soc - ial scene Just a pawn out - played by a dom - inating queen.

159

al - tar bound, hyp - no - tised sweet free - dom whis - pered in my ear. You're a

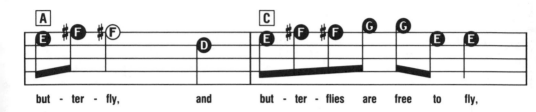

but - ter - fly, and but - ter - flies are free to fly,

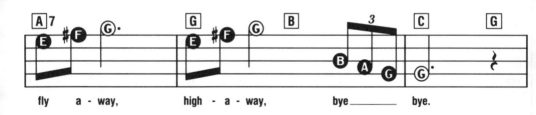

fly a - way, high - a - way, bye_____ bye.

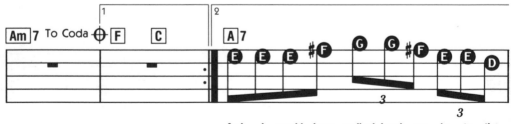

And I would have walked head on in - to the

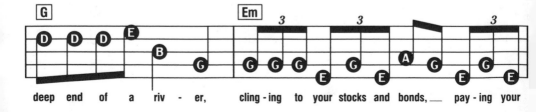

deep end of a riv - er, cling - ing to your stocks and bonds,___ pay - ing your

Sorry Seems To Be The Hardest Word

Regi-Sound Program: 8
Rhythm: 8 Beat or Pops

Words and Music by
Elton John and Taupin

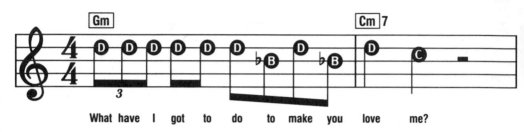

What have I got to do to make you love me?

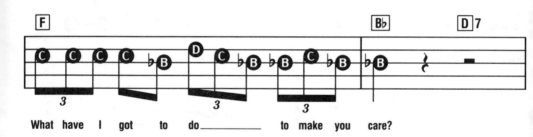

What have I got to do_____ to make you care?

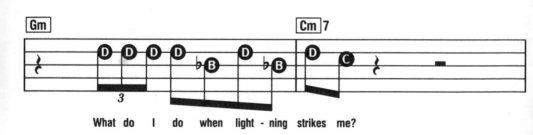

What do I do when light - ning strikes me?

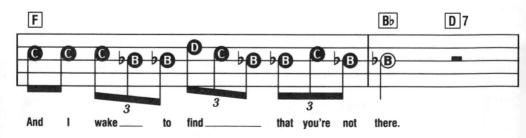

And I wake_____ to find_____ that you're not there.

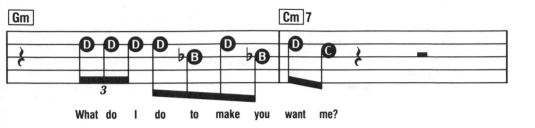

What do I do to make you want me?

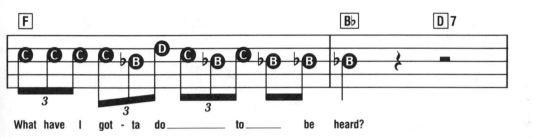

What have I got - ta do_____ to_____ be heard?

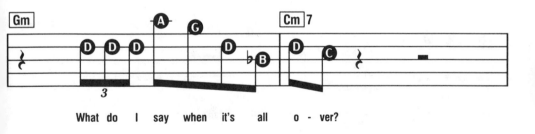

What do I say when it's all o - ver?

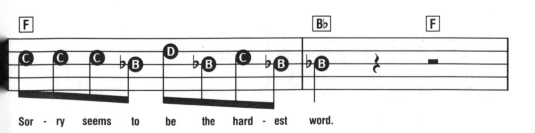

Sor - ry seems to be the hard - est word.

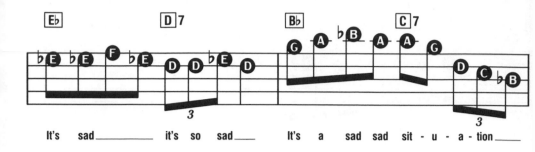

It's sad_____ it's so sad____ It's a sad sad sit - u - a - tion____

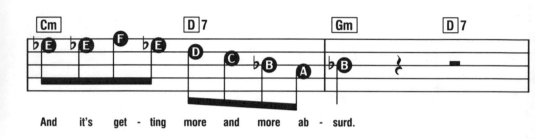

And it's get - ting more and more ab - surd.

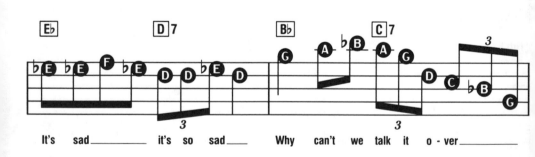

It's sad_____ it's so sad____ Why can't we talk it o - ver_____

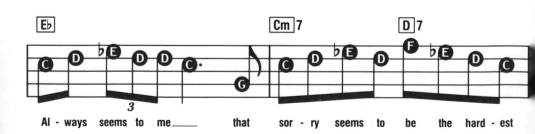

Al - ways seems to me____ that sor - ry seems to be the hard - est

Sweet Painted Lady

Regi-Sound Program: 7
Rhythm: 8 Beat or Pops

Words and Music by
Elton John and Taupin

learned.   If   the   right.   So she   lays down be - side me a - gain. My

sweet   paint - ed   la - dy,   the   one   with   no   name.

Man - y have used her and man - y still do.___   There's a

place in the world for a wom - an like   you.   Oh!

Sweet   paint - ed   la - dy   seems it's al - ways been the same.

Get - ting paid for be - ing layed guess that's the name of the game. Oh!

Guess that's the name of the game. Oh!_____ For - get us we'll have

gone ver - y soon. Just for - get we ev - er slept in your rooms. And

we'll leave the smell of the sea_____ in your beds. Where

love's just a job and noth - ing is said. So she _____

Take Me To The Pilot

Regi-Sound Program: 4
Rhythm: Rock

Words and Music by
Elton John and Taupin

If you feel that it's real I'm on trial, ___ and I'm here ___ in your
know he's not old and I'm told he's a

pris - on, like a coin in your mint, ___ I am
vir - gin, for ___ he may be she, ___ but I'm

dent - ed and spent ___ with ___ high trea - son.⎬
told and I'm nev - er, nev - er for cer - tain.⎬

Through a glass ___ eye, your throne ___ is the one ___ dan - ger zone.

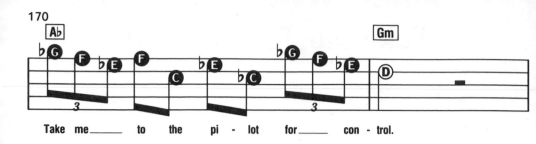

Take me___ to the pi - lot for___ con - trol.

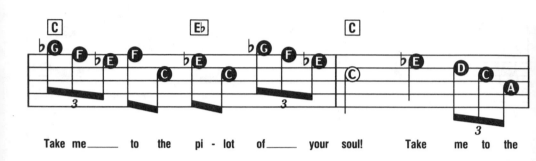

Take me___ to the pi - lot of___ your soul! Take me to the

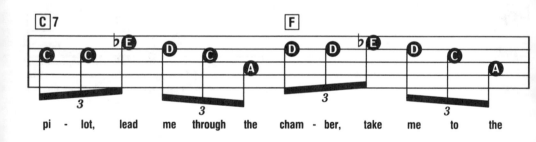

pi - lot, lead me through the cham - ber, take me to the

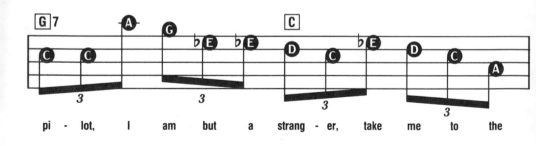

pi - lot, I am but a strang - er, take me to the

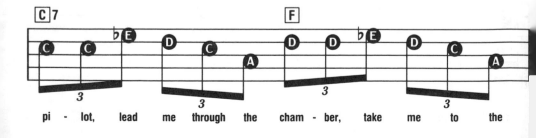

pi - lot, lead me through the cham - ber, take me to the

Tiny Dancer

Regi-Sound Program: 8
Rhythm: 8 Beat or Pops

Words and Music by
Elton John and Taupin

Blue __ jean ba - by, L. _____ A. ___ la - dy,
Je - sus freaks _____ out _____ in the street _____

seam - stress for the band. _____ Pret - ty eyed, _____
hand - ing tick - ets out for God. Turn - ing back _____

pi - rate smile, _____ you'll mar - ry a mu - sic man. _____
she __ just laughs. _____ The bou - le - vard is not that bad.

Bal - le - ri - na. You must have seen her, danc - ing in ____ the
Pi - an - o man ____ he makes his stand ____ in the au - di - to - ri -

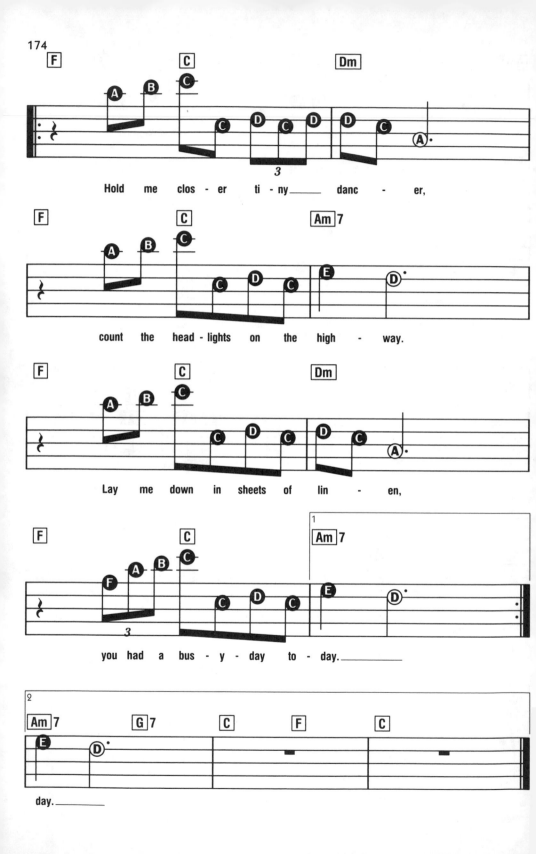

Hold me clos - er ti - ny___ danc - er,

count the head - lights on the high - way.

Lay me down in sheets of lin - en,

you had a bus - y - day to - day.___

day.___

Who Wears These Shoes?

Regi-Sound Program: 7
Rhythm: Rock

Words and Music by
Elton John and Taupin

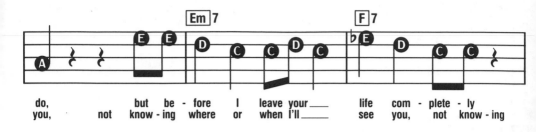

do,   but be - fore   I   leave your____   life   com - plete - ly
you,   not know - ing where   or   when I'll____   see   you,   not know - ing

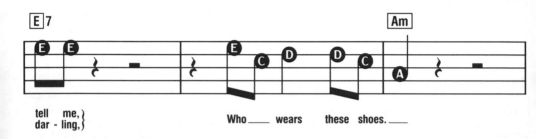

tell   me,   Who____ wears   these shoes.____
dar - ling,

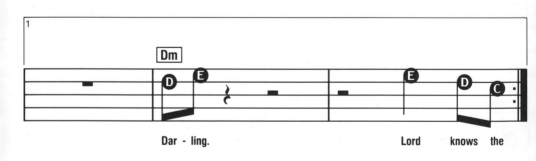

Dar - ling.   Lord   knows the

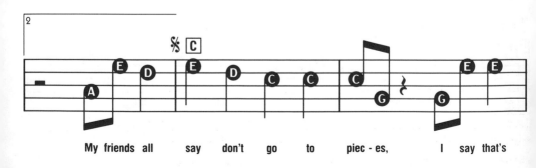

My friends all   say   don't go   to   piec - es,   I say that's

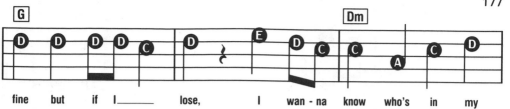

fine   but   if I____   lose,   I   wan - na   know   who's   in   my

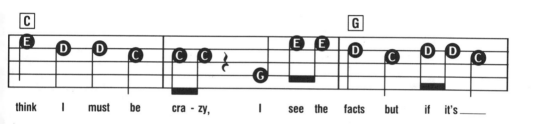

foot - steps,   I   wan - na   know   who   wears   these shoes.____   My   friends   all

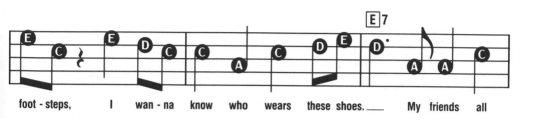

think   I   must   be   cra - zy,   I   see   the   facts   but   if   it's____

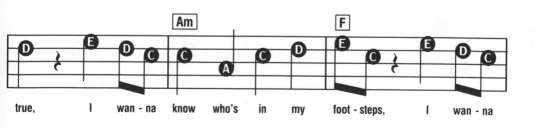

true,   I   wan - na   know   who's   in   my   foot - steps,   I   wan - na

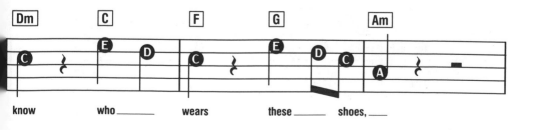

know   who____   wears   these____ shoes,____

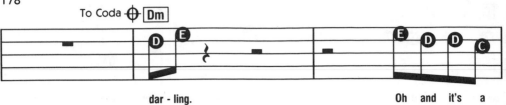
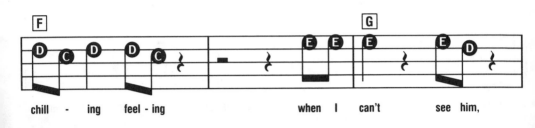
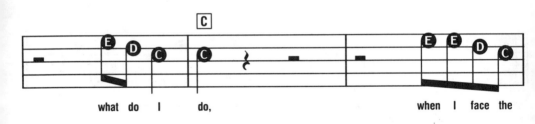
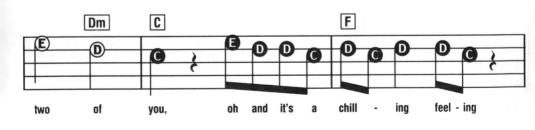
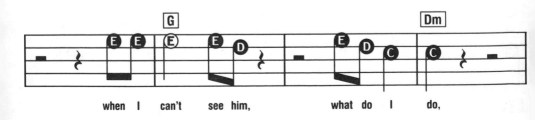

D.S. al Coda
(Return to 𝄋
Play to ⊕ and
skip to Coda)

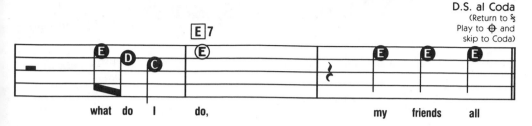

what do I do, my friends all

CODA

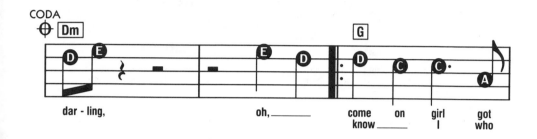

dar - ling, oh, _____ come on girl got
know _____ I who

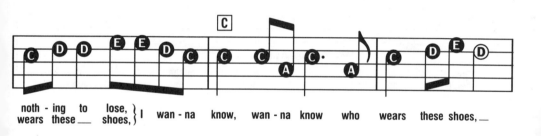

noth - ing to lose, } I wan - na know, wan - na know who wears these shoes, ___
wears these __ shoes,

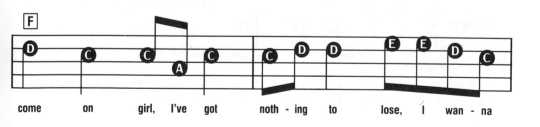

come on girl, I've got noth - ing to lose, I wan - na

Repeat and Fade

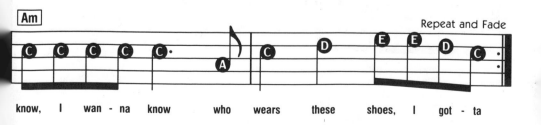

know, I wan - na know who wears these shoes, I got - ta

A Word In Spanish

Regi-Sound Program: 3
Rhythm: 8 Beat or Pops

Words and Music by
Elton John and Taupin

I don't know why,_____ I just know I do,
you can't com - pre - hend,_____ read it in my eyes. If

I just can't ex - plain_____ in this lan - guage that I use.
you don't un - der - stand it's love in a thin dis - guise. And

Some - thing leaves me speech - less, each time that you ap - proach. Each
what it takes to move you, each time that you re - sist, is

time you glide right through me as
more than just a pret - ty face to

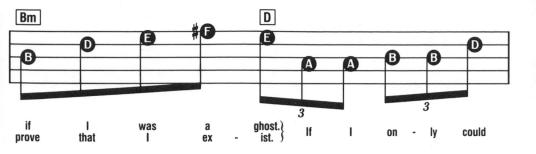

if I was a ghost.}
prove that I ex - ist. } If I on - ly could

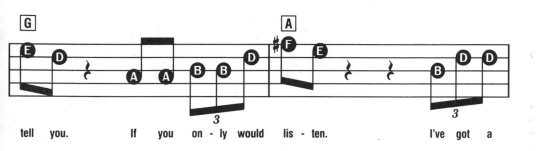

tell you. If you on - ly would lis - ten. I've got a

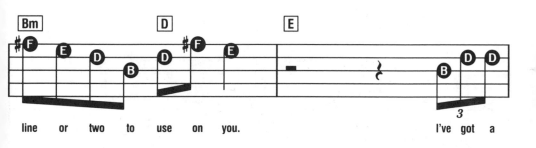

line or two to use on you. I've got a

ro - mance we could christ - en. And there's a word in Span - ish

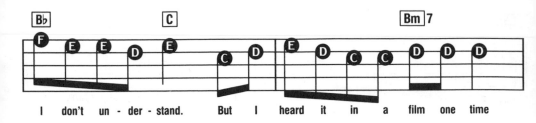

I don't un - der - stand. But I heard it in a film one time

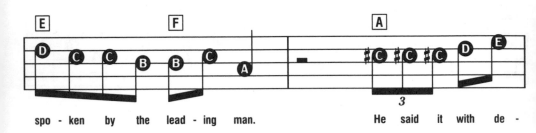

spo - ken by the lead - ing man. He said it with de -

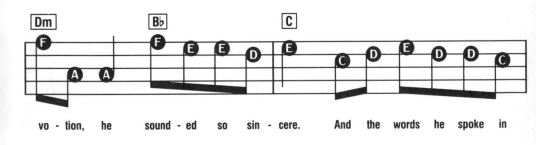

vo - tion, he sound - ed so sin - cere. And the words he spoke in

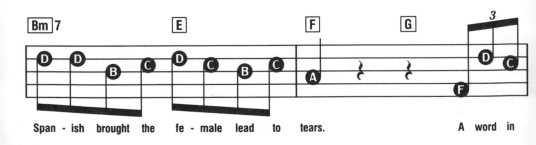

Span - ish brought the fe - male lead to tears. A word in

Wrap Her Up

Regi-Sound Program: 7
Rhythm: Rock

Words and Music by Elton John, Taupin,
Davey Johnstone, Charlie Morgan, Paul Westwood and Fred Mandel

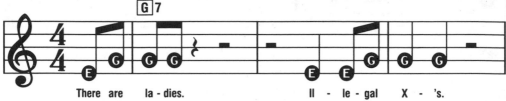

There are la - dies. Il - le - gal X - 's.

Mo - na Li - sas well con - nect - ed.

They may be sha - dy Eng - lish ros - es.

Blue blood - ed, turned up nos - es.

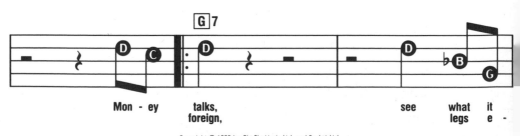

Mon - ey talks, see what it
foreign, legs e -

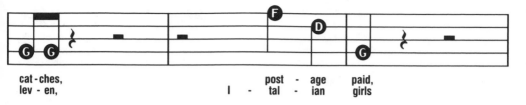

cat - ches,   post - age   paid,
lev - en,   I - tal - ian   girls

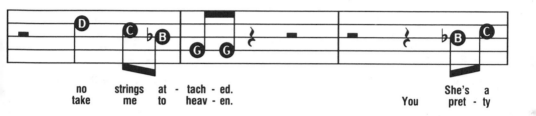

no   strings at - tach - ed.   She's a
take   me to heav - en.   You pret - ty

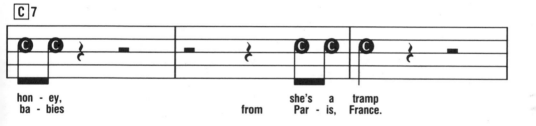

hon - ey,   she's a tramp
ba - bies   from Par - is, France.

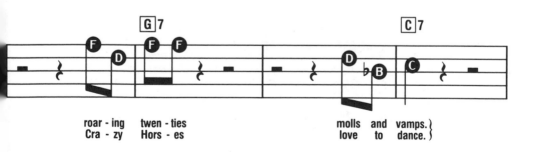

roar - ing twen - ties   molls and vamps. }
Cra - zy Hors - es   love to dance. }

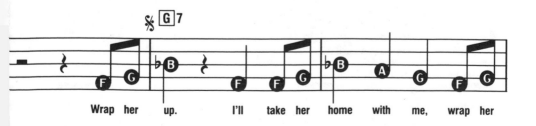

Wrap her up.   I'll take her home with me, wrap her

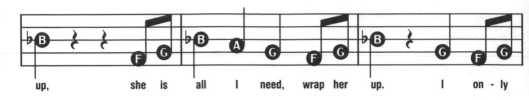

up,   she is   all   I   need, wrap her up.   I   on - ly

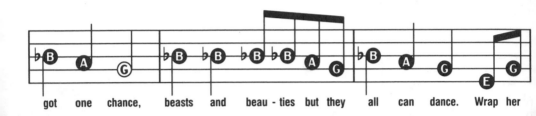

got   one   chance,   beasts   and   beau - ties but they   all   can   dance. Wrap her

C7

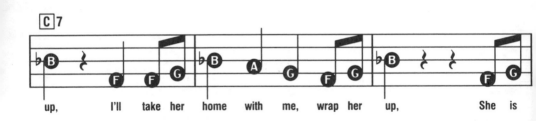

up,   I'll   take her   home   with   me,   wrap her   up,   She is

G7   **C**7

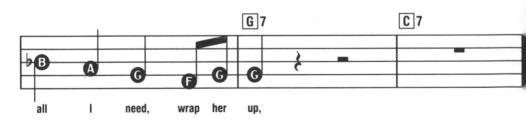

all   I   need,   wrap her   up,

D.S. and Fade

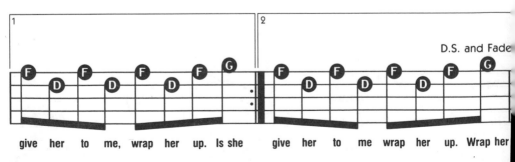

give her   to   me, wrap her up. Is she   give her   to   me wrap her up. Wrap her

Your Sister Can't Twist
(But She Can Rock 'N' Roll)

Regi-Sound Program: 4
Rhythm: Rock

Words and Music by
Elton John and Taupin

I could real - ly get off be - ing in your shoes I used to

be stone sold on rhy - thm and blues. I heard of a place at the

back of town where you real - ly kick the shit when the sun goes down. I

rea - ly got buzzed when your sis - ter said,

"Throw a - way them rec - ords 'cause the blues is dead.

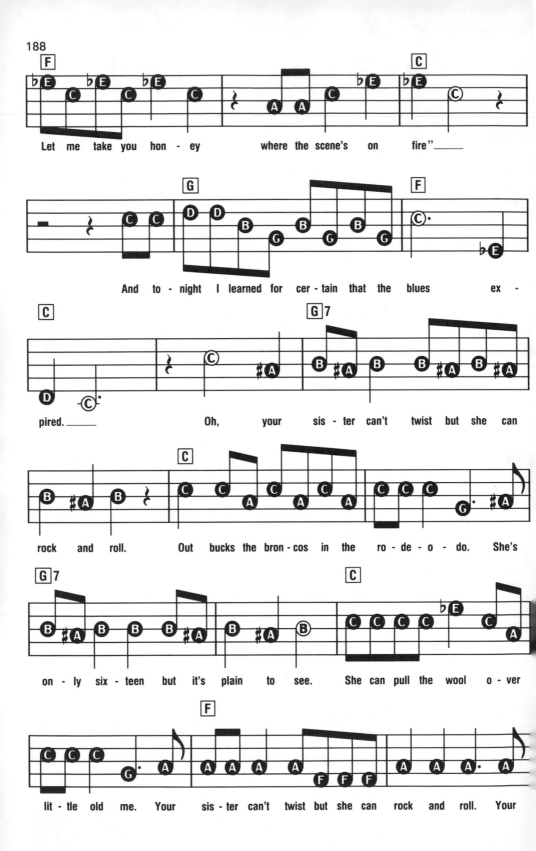

Your Song

Regi-Sound Program: 3
Rhythm: Rock or Jazz Rock

Words and Music by
Elton John and Taupin

It's a lit-tle bit fun-ny this feel-ing in-
If I was a sculp-tor but then a-gain

side, _____ I'm not one of those who can
no, or a man who ____ makes those potions in a

eas-i-ly hide, _____ I don't have much
trav-el-in' show _____ I know ____ it's not

mon - ey, _____ but, boy, if I did. _____
much but it's the best I can do. _____

I'd buy a big house where _____ we both could
My gift is my song and _____

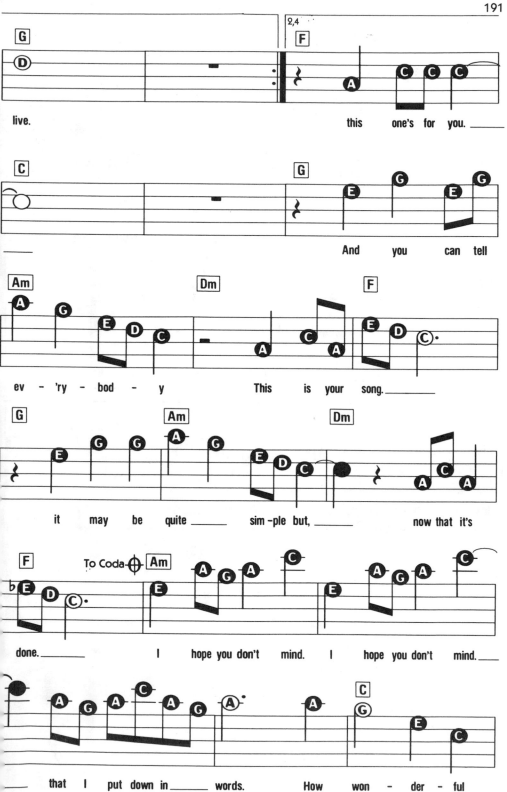

192

life   is   while   You're _____   in   the   world. _____

D.C. al Coda
(Return to beginning,
take 3rd & 4th endings,
Play till ⊕ and skip to Coda)

CODA

I   hope you don't   mind   I   hoipe you don't   mind _____

_____   that   I   put down in _____ words.   How   won – der – ful

life   is   while   you're _____   in   the   world. _____

you're _____ _____   in   the   world. _____

3. I sat on the roof and kicked off the moss.
Well a few of the verses, well they've got me quite cross.
But the sun's been quite kind while I wrote this song,
It's for people like you that keep it turned on.

4. So excuse me forgetting but these things I do
You see I've forgotten if they're green or they're blue,
Anyway the thing is what I really mean
Yours are the sweetest eyes I've ever seen.